CW00497685

The Bequeathmei
Abu Hanifah (may Aɪɪan snow nɪm mercy)

Twelve Principles of Sunni Islamic Belief

By Imam Abu Hanifah al-Numan

Translated and commentated by

Arfan Shah al-Bukhari

Sheikhy Notes

Copyright © Arfan Shah al-Bukhari 2020

Commentary 2020

Translated and commentated by

Arfan Shah al-Bukhari

Volume 2 of the Abu Hanifah series

Published by Sheikhy Notes

This is from the non-profit book publishing venture known as Sheikhy Notes (charity no. 1163573), from the same person who brought Sheikhy Notes blog to you. Please consider contributing to our activities.

Blog: http://www.sheikhynotes.blogspot.com

Translation blog:
http://www.straighttranslations.blogspot.co.uk/

Copy-editing by Muhammad Ridwaan
(QalamEditing.com)

Contact: sheikhynotescharity@gmail.com

Contents

Translator's introduction

In the name of Allah, the Most Merciful and Most Compassionate; may peace, blessings and salutations be upon our master the Prophet.

This work is a commentary on one of the letters of Abu Hanifah (may Allah show him mercy) to his students about Islamic belief. It highlights twelve principles of Sunni Islam that are of the utmost importance.

When teaching this text I found layers of meaning that needed to be unravelled. So we can see the brilliance of the mind of Abu Hanifah (may Allah show him mercy). In what follows, I have included chapter titles, the original Arabic, the translation and the commentary. This is the second volume of our Abu Hanifah (may Allah show him mercy) series, so please look out for forthcoming books.

There was a manuscript at Al-Azhar which had a different introduction, which appears to be a later addition because it is not present in other versions that we found. It also is not consistent with the writings of Abu Hanifah so it has not been included in the present work.

We hope that Allah accepts this commentary and that students of knowledge benefit from this text.

This is the first commentary of this work done solely in the English language.

هذه وصية الإمام الأعظم أبي حنيفة رضي
الله عنه
بسم الله الرحمن الرحيم

This is the bequeathment of the Great Imam, Abu Hanifah (may Allah be pleased with him)

In the name of Allah, the Most Merciful and Most Compassionate

Translation/commentary begins

أما بعد فهذه وصية من الإمام الأعظم أبي
حنيفة رحمه الله لأصحابه رضوان الله عليهم
أجمعين على مذهب أهل السنة والجماعة

"This is the bequeathment of the Great Imam, Abu Hanifah, may Allah show him and his students mercy and may He be pleased with them,

8

according to the *madhhab* of Ahl al-Sunnah wa al-Jama'ah."

Commentary

There are many works by Abu Hanifah, most of them small tracts, epistles and bequests. Yet the depth and strength in them is immense, for which reason he is called the Great Imam from the Salaf, because he was born in that time. All the Hanafis enter into this prayer (*du'a*) in the hope that following a *madhhab* is like following preserved practice of the religion.

We have written an article about *who the Ahl al-Sunnah wa al-Jama'ah* are and it is available on the Sheikhy Notes blog. When we say "may Allah be pleased" for someone who is not a Companion then it is like a prayer for them and we are not comparing them to the Companions.

لما مرض أبو حنيفة رضي الله عنه قال:
اعلموا أصحابي وإخواني إن مذهب أهل السنة
والجماعة على اثنتي عشرة خصلة

"When Abu Hanifah (may Allah be pleased with him) fell [severely] ill, he said, 'My companions and brothers, know that the way of Ahl al-Sunnah wa al-Jama'ah is based on twelve principles."

Commentary

Abu Hanifah (may Allah show him mercy) fell ill, so we are presuming he made this bequest before he died and one of his students copied it down. "He said" indicates that it was a dictation. This is similar to *al-'Aqidah al-Tahawiyyah* because that, too, is a dictated work of Abu Hanifah (may Allah show him mercy).

"Know" is a command form of the verb: "know, my companions and my brothers." "My companions" might be a reference to his students, and "brothers" his peers at the time. They are plural, which includes both genders.

Then he said that there are twelve principles which someone needs to believe in, in order to be counted from the Ahl al-Sunnah wa al-Jama'ah.

فمن كان يستقيم على هذه الخصال لا يكون مبتدعا ولا صاحب هوى فعليكم بهذه الخصال

حتى تكونوا في شفاعة نبينا محمد صلى الله
عليه وسلم يوم القيامة

"Whoever is steadfast on this will not be an innovator or a modernist; so it is necessary for you [to believe in] these attributes to attain the intercession of the Prophet (may Allah bestow peace and blessings upon him)."

Commentary

So if someone is steadfast on this then they will not become an innovator or modernist and thus will attain the intercession of the Prophet (may Allah bestow peace and blessings upon him). There are also forty hadith on the intercession compiled by Sheikh Yusuf al-Nabhani and there is also a work by Imam Ahmed Rida Khan (may Allah show them mercy) on the same subject. Sheikh Yusuf's book has been published by Sheikhy Notes.

The intercession of the Prophet (may Allah bestow peace and blessings upon him) is denied by the Wahhabis and Mu'tazilites and this is another point that separates them from Ahl al-Sunnah. Seeing as there are over forty hadith and even if they were all weak (da'if), they would strengthen each other and become acceptable by another hadith (*hasan li-ghayrihi*), not to mention that there are *sahih* hadiths on this issue.

Al-Subki (may Allah show him mercy) said in *Shifa' al-Saqim*, "Hadiths about the intercession are many and all together they reach a level of mass transmission. Meaning there is no doubt in the narrations about the intercession including any single word of the hadiths. These types of mass transmission of the Sunnah are many. As for mass transmission by words of the texts, this is rare."

Anas and Jabir (may Allah be pleased with them) narrate that the Messenger of Allah (may Allah bestow peace and blessings upon him) said,

شفاعتي لأهل الكبائر من امتي

"My intercession is for the perpetrators of major wrong actions from my nation."[1]

The Mu'tazilites, however, use a single Quranic verse in isolation that says there is no intercession for anyone, but ignore other hadiths.

---

[1] Abu Dawud; al-Bazzar; al-Tabarani from Anas; Ibn Hibban in his *Sahih*; and al-Bayhaqi.

First point: The affirmation of faith

[أولها] الإيمان، وهو إقرار باللسان وتصديق بالجنان

"The first is faith, which is through affirmation with one's tongue and belief in one's heart."

Commentary

Please note the numbers of each point have been added and are not part of the original text but make it easy for the reader to know which point they are on.

Abu Hanifah (may Allah show him mercy) was the first to define faith saying that it is belief in the heart with affirmation on the tongue. The Ash'aris added acting upon the five pillars of Islam as part of faith. Imam Maturidi (may Allah show him mercy) gave a different possibility of faith, that someone could have belief in their heart but not having confirmed it on their tongue. The latter is a believer with Allah (the Exalted) but not in terms of the legal rulings of this world. Another

13

definition is belief in everything that the Messenger (may Allah bestow peace and blessings upon him) brought that is decisive (*qat'i*). Decisive means something well authenticated.

Other groups outside Sunni Islam have their own definitions, such as the Shia, who say one must affirm their Twelve Imams and so forth. Abu Hanifah (may Allah show him mercy) was the first to give a definition of faith and everyone who followed him used this as a building block.

The Khawarij said that those who commit major sins leave Islam, and have to repeat the Testimony of Faith. While the Ash'aris maintain that acting upon the pillars of Islam is included in faith, they do not say that it causes disbelief if one does not practise the five pillars.

This opinion has been resurrected recently by a group who encourage people to practise. They warn people that if they do no practise Islam, they are not Muslim. This is very problematic and obviously the wrong opinion. Sins harm someone and that it without a doubt, but only some sins cause disbelief.

Realisation

ومعرفة بالقلب والإقرار وحده لا يكون إيمانا
لأنه لو كان إيمانا لكان المنافقون كلهم مؤمنين

"Realisation is through one's heart, while affirmation [of one's tongue] alone is not faith, because, were it the case, the hypocrites, one and all, would have been believers."

Commentary

The realisation of the heart and the affirmation means that they necessarily come together and cannot be separated. A *fasiq* is someone who commits sins but there is faith in his heart – so the issue is with his action not his faith.

A *munafiq* manifests faith but is, in fact, devoid of it, and might even commit some good actions. The *fasiq* has faith but in a reduced state. Imam al-Ghazali (may Allah be pleased with him) said the word *munafiq* refers to a mouse that looked as though it was coming out of one hole but came out of a different one completely. The Quran tells us that the hypocrites are in the lowest level of hell because they had faith on their tongues but not in their hearts.

وكذلك المعرفة وحدها لا تكون إيمانا لأنها لو كانت إيمانا لكان أهل الكتاب كلهم مؤمنين قال الله تعالى في حق المنافقين وَاللَّهُ يَشْهَدُ إِنَّ الْمُنَافِقِينَ لَكَاذِبُونَ وقال في حق أهل الكتاب الَّذِينَ آتَيْنَاهُمُ الْكِتَابَ يَعْرِفُونَهُ كَمَا يَعْرِفُونَ أَبْنَاءَهُمْ

"Similarly, realisation alone does not constitute faith because, were it the case, the People of the Book (Ahl al-Kitab), one and all, they [hypocrites] had faith then all of the people of the book would have been believers. Allah (the Exalted) said concerning the hypocrites, 'Allah testifies that the hypocrites are [true] liars.'[2] He said, concerning the People of the Book, 'Those to whom We gave the Book know him like they know their own sons.'"[3]

Commentary

---

[2] Quran: al-Munafiqun 63:1.
[3] Quran: al-Baqarah 2:146.

The Ahl al-Kitab are the Christians, Jews and the Sabians who believed in Yahya (upon him be peace). They are to be respected as well as all non-Muslims. The main difference between Islam and other religions is the affirmation of divinity being with Allah alone and belief in the final messenger Muhammad (may Allah bestow peace and blessings upon him). Here Abu Hanifah (may Allah show him mercy) states the importance of utterance with the knowing of the heart, just like the Testification of faith (*kalima tayyiba*) comprises two parts of a whole.

The hypocrites lie with the sins by their limbs. They will be in the lowest level of hell because they knew and denied the truth. The verse speaks about those who came to the Prophet (may Allah bestow peace and blessings upon him) feigning belief but were really liars. So this adds more evidence to Abu Hanifah's (may Allah show him mercy) claim that faith is belief in the heart combined with affirmation on the tongue. Here the hypocrites had faith on their tongues but not in their hearts, and so this again validates the description of faith by Abu Hanifah (may Allah show him mercy). Also, note that action was not mentioned and so the Hanafis do not consider action to be part of faith.

The People of the Book knew that the Prophet (may Allah bestow peace and blessings upon him) was true and knew his description as they knew their own sons but still rejected him. The Torah and the Injil included descriptions of the Prophet (may Allah bestow peace and blessings upon him) and his Companions. There is a book called *Muhammad in the Bible* by Abdul Ahad Dawud which discusses each place where the Prophet (may Allah bestow peace and blessings upon him) is mentioned. The song of Solomon in the Bible is the first description of the Prophet (may Allah bestow peace and blessings upon him), where there is a line translated as "altogether he is lovely" but in Hebrew the name *Muhammadim* is mentioned; "*-im*" is a suffix of respect in Hebrew, so if we take that away then we are left with "Muhammad" (may Allah bestow peace and blessings upon him).

They truly knew the Prophet (may Allah bestow peace and blessings upon him) like they did their own sons. Knowledge is meant to be acted upon and not ignored. Yet many Jews and Christians did accept Islam in that time, which is a testimony to them following the true reports of a final messenger. Let it be known that we do not disrespect people belonging to other religious traditions ever. Why? If you curse them, they will curse Islam, and this is what the hadith that mentions not cursing one's father is about. When one curses someone's father then someone will curse your father as a result.

Faith increases and decreases

والإيمان لا يزيد ولا ينقص لأنه لا يتصور
نقصانه إلا بزيادة الكفر ولا يتصور زيادته إلا
بنقصان الكفر

"Faith does not increase or decrease because it's unimaginable that it should decrease without one increasing in disbelief; and it's unimaginable that it should increase without one decreasing in disbelief."

Commentary

This is a classical point of disagreement between the Ash'aris and Hanafis. The Ash'aris say that faith can increase and decrease but the Hanafis and Maturidis maintain that it cannot. Imam al-Shafi'i (may Allah be pleased with him) said that faith can increase and decrease.[4]

The Hanafis say the faith that every believer has is the same. The Maturidis agree but add that one does not have to verbalise it. The Ash'aris say that

---

[4] Imam al-Nasafi, *Bahr al-Kalam*, p. 85.

there are three such levels: faith of the prophets, which can increase but not decrease; faith of the angels, which does not increase or decrease;[5] and faith of mankind or jinn, which can increase or decrease.

Abu Hanifah (may Allah show him mercy) said, "My faith is *like* the faith of Jibril but I do not say *similar* to the faith of Jibril," meaning that the articles of faith they all believe in are the same but not the quality of the faith, which is not the same. The faith of the angels is something that is gifted to them by Allah (the Exalted). Similarly, they can only obey Allah (the Exalted) as they do not have the propensity to disobey.

The Ash'aris will point to the following verse as to the reason why faith can increase:

$$ لِيَزْدَادُوٓا۟ إِيمَـٰنًا مَّعَ إِيمَـٰنِهِمْ $$

"...that they would increase in their faith along with their [present] faith."[6] Imam Abu Layth al-Samarqandi (may Allah show him mercy) said, "It [the verse] means truthfulness with the truthfulness they already possessed." All the verses that

[5] al-Bajuri.
[6] Quran: al-Fath 48:4.

mention that there is an increase in faith mean that there is an increase in certainty and truthfulness, as stated by Imam al-Samarqandi (may Allah show him mercy) about Quran 8:2, "…they increased in faith." Other verses include 9:124, 74:31, 47:18 and so on.

Al-Khatabi (may Allah show him mercy) said, "Faith is speech that does not increase. Action increases and decreases. Belief increases and does not increase; if it decreases, then it leaves."[7] "Leaves" meaning disbelief occurs.

Imam al-Ghazali (may Allah show him mercy) mentions in his *Ihya' 'Ulum al-Din* under the principles of faith, about the increase and decrease of faith, that "there is a proof that action is not a part of faith and the pillars. Rather there is an increase of it not with it. The increase and decrease is on something present and not an increase of its essence. It is not possible to say that mankind increases by his head; rather, we say that it increases by a beard or plumpness. It is not possible to say prayer increases by prostration and bowing; rather, we say it increases by manners and Sunnah. It is clear that faith is present, then after its presence, does it differ in its state of increase and decrease" (p. 171). The Imam has taken a

---

[7] *Hashiyah al-Sawi*, p. 138.

position with the Maturidis and Hanafis here, which is interesting because he is, for the most part, Ash'ari. He says that actions are not part of faith but are extra.

The hadiths about a person not being a believer whilst he fornicates or steals should be taken as warnings not to do such things. For if faith was to leave one, then one would be a disbeliever. Though it is very important to note that faith can only be voluntarily surrendered and not taken.

It is not possible for the prophets (upon them be peace) to commit disbelief before or after prophethood.

ءَامَنَ ٱلرَّسُولُ بِمَآ أُنْزِلَ إِلَيْهِ مِن رَّبِّهِ وَٱلْمُؤْمِنُونَ كُلٌّ آمَنَ بِٱللَّهِ وَمَلَائِكَتِهِ وَكُتُبِهِ وَرُسُلِهِ

"The messengers believed in what was sent by their Lord and the believers all have faith in Allah, His angels, His books and His messengers."[8] This verse is proof that the messengers and prophets believed and, in its past tense meaning, they "believed" whatever was revealed by Allah (the Exalted). They were never in a state of rejection of faith, and whoever claims otherwise has gone

---

[8] Quran: al-Baqarah 2:285.

against scholarly consensus (*ijma'*) on this matter. The faith of the prophets (upon them be peace) is affirmed and untouchable. They are our masters and leaders in faith.

Imam al-Sanusi (may Allah be pleased with him) said, "There is consensus (*ijma'*) of the people of the truth about the faith of the prophets and messengers (upon them all be peace) and they are free from sins and errors. The most virtuous and the master of them, indeed the most virtuous of all creation, is our master and our prophet Muhammad (may Allah bestow peace and blessings upon him)."[9] The Imam confirms that there is consensus that the prophets and messengers had faith, including before and after prophethood and that they are free from sins.

The Ash'aris say that the faith of the prophets increases and does not decrease, although the Maturidis disagree, as mentioned by Abu Hanifah (may Allah be pleased with him).

Regarding the verse "Do you not believe?"[10] Imam al-Bajuri (may Allah be pleased with him) said it means, "Does not your faith suffice?" – faith

---

[9] Imam Muhammad al-Sanusi, *Sharh al-Muqadimmah*, p. 169.
[10] Quran: al-Baqarah 2:260.

meaning certainty and that there was increase in a level of certainty.

Abu Bakr's (may Allah be pleased with him) faith was weightier than the faith of others of the Ummah, for it was the quality not quantity. Imam al-Nasafi said, "It [Abu Bakr's faith] is weightier in reward because he excelled [others] in faith."[11]

On the Day of Judgement, those with even the quality of a mustard seed of faith will be taken out of hell.

---

[11] Imam al-Nasafi, *Bahr al-Kalam*, p. 86.

A believer or disbeliever, not both at the same time!

وكيف يجوز أن يكون الشخص الواحد في حالة
واحدة مؤمنا وكافرا والمؤمن مؤمن حقا
والكافر كافر حقا وليس في الإيمان شك كما أن
ليس في الكفر شك لقوله تعالى أُولَٰئِكَ هُمُ
الْمُؤْمِنُونَ حَقًّا وأُولَٰئِكَ هُمُ الْكَافِرُونَ حَقًّا

"How is it conceivable for any given person in any given moment to be a believer and disbeliever at the same time, or a true believer and a true disbeliever? There is no doubt in faith, just as there is no doubt in disbelief, in view of the Exalted having said, 'Those are true believers,'[12] and, 'Those are true disbelievers.'"[13]

Commentary

---

[12] Quran: al-Anfal 8:4.
[13] Quran: al-Nisa' 4:151.

A person cannot be a believer and a disbeliever at one and the same time. At a specific moment in time, states cannot be the same; only one quality, or another, can inhere. Something can be of a high standard or not, but it cannot be of both poor and high quality at the same time in totality. There cannot be a percentage of belief in a person. It is either full or none. He should have no doubt in his faith. This is found by studying texts of belief until there is no doubt or question. If someone has a doubt then he must find an answer straight away. Similarly, a disbeliever has no faith and is certain of his disbelief. How strange it is when two people look at the same thing and one derives faith from it, and the other derives disbelief!

The above verse in reference to the true believers describes those who pray and give charity.[14] The true disbelievers, by contrast, are described as follows:

إِنَّ ٱلَّذِينَ يَكْفُرُونَ بِٱللَّهِ وَرُسُلِهِ وَيُرِيدُونَ أَن يُفَرِّقُواْ بَيْنَ ٱللَّهِ وَرُسُلِهِ وَيَقُولُونَ نُؤْمِنُ بِبَعْضٍ وَنَكْفُرُ بِبَعْضٍ وَيُرِيدُونَ أَن يَتَّخِذُواْ بَيْنَ ذَٰلِكَ سَبِيلاً

---

[14] See note 12.

"Those who disbelieve in Allah and His Messenger; they want to separate between Allah and His Messenger; they say they will believe in part and disbelief in part; they want to adopt this [misguided] path."[15] This also serves as evidence for Abu Hanifah's (may Allah show him mercy) position that a person cannot be part believer and thus part disbeliever. The misguided people want to believe in Allah and not the Messenger, but that is still disbelief. In order for belief to occur, both parts of the Testification of Faith have to be present: confirmation of the Divine and prophethood. Then the next verse confirms these as true disbelievers because they affirmed part of faith and rejected another part. Note that action is not mentioned as a part of faith here. The verse affirms both parts of faith but mentions nothing of action.

There is disagreement among scholars about whether saying "I am a Muslim, if Allah wills" affirms one's faith. The Hanafis and Maturidis would say that if asked whether you are Muslim, you must simply say, "I am Muslim," and not "if Allah wills", because we have to be certain in it. Hasan al-Basri (may Allah be pleased with him) and others of the Salaf used to say "if Allah wills" (*in sha' Allah*). Imam al-Ghazali (may Allah show

---

him mercy) notes four uses of the term *in sha'
Allah*: the first two are connected with doubt; the
third is connected to manners of the remembrance
of Allah (*dhikr*); and the last is connected to doubt
and the time of death.[16] Another definition that he
provides is that *in sha' Allah* is used to manifest
desire (*raghbah*) and hope (*tamanni*). We would
say that the early Salaf, the Muslims from the first
to the third century and excluding anyone else,
used to say it in hope and desire of dying a
Muslim. The Ash'aris could be saying *in sha'
Allah* for any of the linguistic meanings above.

The Hanafis would say "I am a Muslim" in
certainty in their belief but being aware that only
Allah knows one's true end. We can say it in hope
and desire of dying as Muslims, without any
presence of doubt. Doubt is the difference between
the Ash'aris and us in this matter.

If someone says, "I am a Muslim, if Allah wills,"
we should not rebuke them based on doubt. Nor
should we accuse someone who says "I am a
Muslim" of thereby being cognisant of the
knowledge of Allah.

---

[16] Imam al-Ghazali, *Ihya' 'Ulum al-Din*, Book of Principles of Faith, p.
173–5.

In our time, the term "if Allah wills" is often used to mean "I might do something or I might not, depending on what I choose."

Muslims who commit major sins

والعاصون من أمة محمد عليه السلام كلهم
مؤمنون حقا وليسوا بكافرين والعمل غير
الإيمان والإيمان غير العمل بدليل أن كثيرا من
الأوقات يرتفع العمل عن المؤمن

"The sinners of the nation of Muhammad, upon him be peace, are all true believers and not disbelievers. Action is not faith and nor is faith action, and a proof for this is that most of the time action is removed from the believer."

Commentary

This follows on to what is known as the disagreement of a sinner when he dies. Does he die Muslim or not? According to the Khawarij, the sinner dies in disbelief and the Mu'tazilites say he is between heaven and hell. Both opinions are rejected by Ahl al-Sunnah.

A person who commits major sins is still a believer but sinful.

31

قال الطحاوي رحمه الله: ولا نكفر أحداً من
أهل القبلة بذنب ما لم يستحله

Imam al-Tahawi (may Allah be pleased with him) said in *al-'Aqida al-Tahawiyyah*, "We do not apostatise anyone of those who pray to Makkah because of sin; as long as they do not deem it lawful." This was originally sourced from *Fiqh al-Akbar* from Abu Hanifah (may Allah be pleased with him). *Al-'Aqida al-Tahawiyyah* is Abu Hanifah's work dictated by his students.

Committing any major sin does not make one a disbeliever unless he believes that the sin is lawful. If he thinks it is halal to eat pork, drink wine/alcohol, fornicate illegally or bet, he is a disbeliever.

Note that a Muslim might be asleep and he is not busy doing good actions but we still describe him as a Muslim. Therefore, action is not part of faith because the sleeping Muslim is still a Muslim.

Action is not faith and nor is faith action. You might come across someone who had wonderful actions but is a disbeliever and you might come across a believer who is committing evil actions.

How do you look at this bizarre event? Suhayl ibn Sa'd (may Allah be pleased with him) narrates that the Messenger of Allah (may Allah bestow peace and blessings upon him) said, "The servant will perform the actions of the residents of the fire while they are from the residents of paradise, and (others) they will perform the actions of the residents of paradise while they are from the residents of the fire. Actions are only finished once completed."[17]

This is evidence that a person will not be judged on action alone rather he will be judged on faith. If he has done a lot of evil then he will have to spend some time in hell. A moment in hell will make someone forget all the pleasures they had experienced in their lives. It also indicates that action alone does not enter one into paradise; rather, it is faith that makes one enter paradise. Some people become confused with disbelievers doing good actions but it is their faith that matters.

---

[17] Bukhari 11/499; Muslim 1/106 without "Actions are only finished once completed".

Faith and action

ولا يجوز أن يقال ارتفع عنه الإيمان فأن الحائض يرفع الله سبحانه تعالى عنها الصلاة ولا يجوز أن يقال رفع الله عنها الإيمان أو أمرها بترك الإيمان وقد قال لها الشرع دع الصوم ثم اقضيه ولا يجوز أن يقال دع الإيمان ثم اقضيه ويجوز أن يقال ليس على الفقير الزكاة ولا يجوز أن يقال ليس على الفقير الإيمان

"It is not possible to say that faith has been lifted from one like Allah, Glorious and Exalted, has lifted [the obligation of] prayer from a woman in her menses. Nor is it permissible to say that Allah has raised faith from her or ordered her to leave faith. Rather, the sacred law has enjoined her to forgo fasting but make it up. Nor is it permissible to say leave faith then make it up. It is permissible to say that [payment of] zakat is not [obligatory] for the poor, but it is not permissible to say there is [no need] for the poor to have faith."

34

Commentary

There is a so much meaning here that even a few volumes would not suffice. Allah (the Exalted) does not take the faith out of someone; it is they who surrender it to the devil, for the sake of this world. The points we have mentioned would make people blame Allah (the Exalted) for their lack of faith, when it is their fault for mixing with the disbelievers and their opinions until delusion overcomes their hearts with darkness. The example of a woman in her menses, or postpartum period, serves to illustrate that the obligations of prayer and fasting are lifted from her but as soon as she is better, she make up the fasts though not the prayers.

It is easier to make up fasts once a year rather than ten days of prayer every thirty days. Note that faith and action are not forced upon anyone, because there would be no point to reward or punishment. Reward and punishment are based on one's choice.

To force someone to utter the Testimony of Faith is not allowed and not accepted; nor is it acceptable to make a non-Muslim repeat it because this has no effect without being conjoined with faith in the heart. It is they who should say it themselves without any coercion.

لا إِكْرَاهَ فِى ٱلدّين

"There is no compulsion in religion." Imam al-Nasafi (may Allah be show him mercy) said, "There is no forcing the religion of truth; namely, the religion of Islam." The Shafiʿis also consider that an act of worship can be forced. The Hanafis, however, take this verse as related to belief not action.

If someone is forced to utter words of disbelief then it is also not valid. If a person is forced by gunpoint, to save their life, to utter the words of disbelief then he may, with the condition that his faith is not weak.

Zakat is only to be paid by those who have more than the *nisab* (threshold) of 100 grams of gold or 700 grams of silver. Otherwise, they might be eligible to receive zakat. The poor do not pay zakat and are instead eligible for it but they are expected to have faith in order to receive it. Faith is not about money or a lack thereof; rather, it is about the truth.

The person in real poverty has lots of money and has no faith in Allah and His Messenger (may Allah bestow peace and blessings upon him). This section gives us a description about action and faith. Faith is permanent and action is dependent on circumstances.

Please note a woman in her menses is rewarded for not praying, because she is obeying the command that came to her.

Good and evil

وتقدير الخير والشر كله من الله سبحانه
وتعالى لأن لو زعم أحد أن تقدير الخير والشر
من غيره لصار كافرا بالله وبطل توحيده إن
كان له توحيد

"The decree of good and evil is all created by
Allah, Glorified and Exalted, and so if someone
was to claim that anyone besides Him has the
ability to decree good and evil, he would become a
disbeliever in Allah and nullify any monotheism
that he had."

Commentary

وَخَلَقَ كُلَّ شَيْءٍ فَقَدَّرَهُ تَقْدِيراً

"He created every living thing and decreed
everything for them."[18] The Mu'tazilites claim that
the servant creates his own actions but this is a
rejected opinion because, how can the servant

---

[18] Quran: al-Furqan 25:2.

create actions himself? That would mean something happens without the prior knowledge of Allah and inside His dominion. This makes Allah weak or compelled to accept the decision of someone; rather, this is baseless. Allah is the creator of decree and has the power to compel all living things to His will whether they like it or not. Allah created everything and has already decreed its provision, its lifespan and its death. This is the same for every living thing and this is not difficult for Him.

The good returns to Allah and the evil is because of what our hands have earned. This is the basis for reward and punishment. We are not forced to do good or evil; rather, it is our choice. Allah already knows what we will choose before we have made the choice.

Christian theologians are faced with the issue called *the problem of evil*, which is the question of how to reconcile the existence of evil and suffering with an omnipotent, omnibenevolent and omniscient God. The question they are often asked is: if God is good then why is there evil in the world? From an Islamic point of view, we understand God/Allah by understanding the Quran and the Sunnah. To learn more, we can see how the ninety-nine wonderful Names of Allah (the

Exalted) relate to us and our lives. To say that 'if God is all powerful then why does He not rid the world of suffering?' is a silly question because only paradise is meant to have no suffering and pain; and this world is not paradise. Allah is not weak and the absence of good does not mean an absence of God. When evil is committed in the world then it is man or jinn at fault and they will be punishable on the Day of Judgement. Man makes his own choices, and had Allah forced people to do good all the time, there would be no basis for reward, because it would not be due to his choice or free will.

Allah (the Exalted) will take revenge from the evil-doers and hell will be their abode. Most atheists do not realise that the Day of Judgement is when the tyrants will be destroyed and tormented by the people they killed. Therefore, there is no *problem of evil* in Islam, but rather there is a *problem in understanding*.

Going to a sacred place to supplicate, a grave of a *wali* (saint) or asking someone to pray for you is permissible and rewardable. The special places of Makkah, Medinah, graves of the prophets and *awliya* and so on – these all have a sacredness that is not found elsewhere. The graves of the disbelievers are dark and they are being punished until they receive worse in hell. The graves of the believers are special places.

The Messenger of Allah (may Allah bestow peace and blessings upon him) said,

القبر إما روضة من رياض الجنة أو حفر من حفر النار

"The grave is either one of the gardens of paradise or one of the pits of hell" (Tirmidhi). This hadith confirms that the graves of the prophets and righteous are special places and that is why supplication is accepted there. Note that punishment in the grave is mass transmitted, which means rejecting it causes disbelief. Also worth noting is that we pray to Allah and not to the prophet or the *wali*.

وَلَوْ أَنَّهُمْ إِذ ظَّلَمُوٓاْ أَنْفُسَهُمْ جَآءُوكَ فَٱسْتَغْفَرُواْ ٱللَّهَ وَٱسْتَغْفَرَ لَهُمُ ٱلرَّسُولُ لَوَجَدُواْ ٱللَّهَ تَوَّاباً رَّحِيماً

"If they came to you after they had wronged themselves and sought the forgiveness of Allah and the Messenger sought forgiveness for them;

41

Allah would be merciful to them and accept their repentance."[19]

Imam al-Qurtubi (may Allah show him mercy) said in his Quranic commentary,

وَلَوْ أَنَّهُمْ إذ ظَّلَمُوٓاْ أَنْفُسَهُمْ جَآءُوكَ روى أبو صادق عن عليّ قال: قدم علينا أعرابيّ بعدما دقّنا رسول الله صلى الله عليه وسلم بثلاثة أيام، فرمى بنفسه على قبر رسول صلى الله عليه وسلم، وحَثَّا على رأسه من ترابه فقال: قلتَ يا رسول الله فسمعنا قولك، وَوَعَيْتَ عن الله فوعينا عنك، وكان فيما أنزل الله عليك وَلَوْ أَنَّهُمْ إذ ظَّلَمُوٓاْ أَنْفُسَهُمْ الآية، وقد ظلمتُ نفسي وجئتك تستغفر لي. فنودي من القبر أنه قد غفر لك. ومعنى لَوَجَدُواْ ٱللَّهَ تَوَّاباً رَّحِيماً أي قابلا لتوبتهم، وهما مفعولان لا غير

"'If they came to you after they had wronged themselves': it was reported by Abu Sadiq from 'Ali that he said, 'A Bedouin came to us after the Messenger of Allah (may Allah bestow peace and blessings upon him) was buried three days

_____

[19] Quran: al-Nisa' 4:64.

previously. He threw himself on the grave of the Messenger of Allah (may Allah bestow peace and blessings upon him) and placed his head in the soil and said, "O Messenger of Allah, hear our words, you are heedful about Allah so be heedful to us. Allah has revealed this about you, 'If they came to you after they wronged themselves …' I have wronged myself, so I come to you, asking you to seek forgiveness for me." There was voice heard from the grave, "You are forgiven.'" The meaning of 'Allah would be merciful to them and accept their repentance' is that He will accept their repentance."

This verse proves that it is permissible to go to Medinah, repent and then ask the Prophet (may Allah bestow peace and blessings upon him) to also seek Allah's forgiveness for you. It is a primary proof for asking to be interceded with Allah, which is termed *tawassul*. This verse also proves that asking someone to pray for one is good for them, too. Notice that 'Ali was there and he did not say anything against this man or blame him. No one could contravene the Shariah in the presence of 'Ali (may Allah ennoble his face).

Black magic does not have its own power and most of it is false superstition. The evil eye can have an effect but only by the will of Allah. People are often deluded into thinking that the evil eye and black magic have a power of their own. This is falsehood but some people are often too far gone in their misunderstandings, and this includes fortune-tellers.

Some Hanafi scholars have declared those who practise black magic to be disbelievers and this is to stop people from doing such wretched acts. Most of the Hanafis maintain that black magic is a major sin, but one has to understand that it is mentioned as *kufr* to make people stop doing it. If they believe that it has a power in itself then it is disbelief.

Second point: Classification of actions

و[الثاني] نقر بأن الأعمال ثلاثة: فريضة
وفضيلة ومعصية

"[Second point:] actions are of three categories –
obligatory, virtuous and disobedience."

Commentary

Ibn 'Abidin (may Allah show him mercy) in his
Hashiya (1/70) said, "The [categories of] sacred
law are four: *fard*, *wajib*, *sunnah* and *nafl*." In the
above, Abu Hanifah has included *fard* and *wajib*
together (*faridah*) and *sunnah* and *nafl* together
(*fadilah*).

Obligatory are the five pillars: *shahada*, once in a
lifetime; prayer, five times a day; Hajj; once in a
lifetime; fasting, one month a year; and zakat, once
a year – if you have the money.

Obligatory (*fard*) action is something that if you do
not perform it, makes you sinful. Refusing to

believe in the obligatory nature of *fard* actions is disbelief.

Imam al-Zarnuji (may Allah show him mercy) said in *Ta'lim al-Muta'allim*, "It is obligatory for every Muslims to seek what he needs at his current state, meaning in his present condition. It is necessary for him to prayer, so it is an obligation for him to learn what he needs for the prayer so that he able to [correctly] perform the prayer. It is necessary for him to perform his *wajib* [necessary] actions and what allows you to establish a *wajib* is *wajib* [in itself]."

What that quote means is that anything that helps you perform a *wajib* or a *fard* is also *wajib* to learn. Then the Imam talks about studying things that refine and correct one's character like removing pride and so on, as well as arriving to knowledge of Allah. These are of course the sciences of the heart because there are internal unlawful states of one's character that need to be removed.

Then one has to learn Islamic belief to a level that removes one's doubts as well as learn of the miracles of Islam and the Prophet (may Allah bestow peace and blessings upon him).

Virtuous (*fadilah*) actions are those that are not *fard* or *wajib*, namely, the *sunnah* acts, not connected to the *wajib* or *fard*. These are extra actions that increase one's reward.

There are different types of *sunnah* in fiqh: *sunnah muzabahah* (frequent *sunnah*), which is something rarely left; *sunnah ghayr muzabahah* (infrequent *sunnah*), something done infrequently; *sunnah mu'akkadah and sunnah mustahab*, which are similar to the above definitions (see *Commentary of the Initiation* (Sheikhy Notes, 2018)).

The following is taken from my article *What Is Sunnah*, "The Prophet (may Allah bestow peace and blessings upon him) made things easy for people and would not burden them with actions that they could not perform. So we can differentiate between three types of Sunnah: One the Sunnah [that] adheres one to the commands and avoidance of prohibitions and the Sunnah that is extra, the beautification of actions. The former is more important but people place more importance to the latter. The second Sunnah, if performed is rewarded and not punished if not performed. Like standing under a tree and half of you is in the shade. Not following this Sunnah is not going to send you to hell but it's better if you do it. Do not misunderstand me if you are doing any Sunnah

47

then keep doing it. Three: Sunnahs we are not commanded to do and if we do them, we will be sinful. Marrying more than four women is haram, continually fasting without break and so forth. The Prophet (may Allah bestow peace and blessings upon him) was allowed by Allah (the Exalted) to have more than four wives but this is unlawful for anyone else. Continually fasting will [cause] harm to the body of most people. There are things that the Prophet (may Allah bestow peace and blessings upon him) did that no one can do and these are known as *Khasais*/specific characteristics or actions."

There are extra actions that are *nafl* which can be done, but there is no sin if left and increase one's reward. Extra things like not having half your body in the shade and half in the sun. There is no specific religious command to it and you are not sinful. Or helping people before they ask because you know their circumstances well.

Sins are either major or minor. Some major sins include a penal punishment and some do not. Backbiting, slandering, eating pork and talebearing are all haram but there is no penal punishment for them; likewise lies, unless someone has lied to take the property of another unjustly. Major sins include drinking alcohol/wine, illegal fornication, accusing someone chaste of fornication, *shirk* and so forth. Major sins have mass-transmission level of being in at least one Quranic verse, including hadith, or many of both. Minor sins have a few hadiths about them and some scholars consider them *makruh* (disliked) to perform.

Imam al-Shafi'i (may Allah show him mercy) said, "If your love of Him was true then you would obey Him."

The obligatory

فالفريضة بأمر الله تعالى ومشيئته ومحبته
ورضاه وقضائه وقدره وتخليقه وحكمه وعلمه
وتوفيقه وكتابته في اللوح المحفوظ

"The obligatory is through [following] the command of Allah (the Exalted), His will, His love, His satisfaction, His predestination, His decree, His bringing into existence, His ruling, His knowledge, His given success [to servants] and His record of it in the Lawh al-Mahfuz/Preserved Tablet."

Commentary

The *fard* or *wajib* is a command by Allah (the Exalted) for every single Muslim and that indicates that everyone can perform the five pillars because Allah (the Exalted) would not command the impossible. People who think they cannot do it only do so out of their own weakness. The will of Allah (the Exalted) overcomes all wills and nothing happens except what He wills.

$$\text{وَمَا تَشَآءُونَ إِلَّا أَن يَشَآءَ ٱللَّهُ رَبُّ ٱلْعَالَمِينَ}$$

"You do not will except what Allah wills: the Sustainer of all creation."[20] Imam al-Qurtubi (may Allah show him mercy) said in his commentary, "By this it is clear that the servant does not do any good [actions] except by the support of Allah and does not evil except that he is misguided. I swear by Allah, that the Arabs did not accept Islam until Allah willed it. Wahb ibn Munabbih [may Allah show him mercy] said, '[This statement was] in eighty-seven books that Allah sent to His prophets.'"

$$\text{يُحِبُّهُمْ وَيُحِبُّونَهُ}$$

"He loves them and they love Him."[21] This verse is about Allah's love for the believers. He loves them and they love Him. So if you love Allah then Allah loves you but the love of Allah was first. Allah's love for the believers was present before any of us were born. Ponder that for a moment and bathe in this powerful blessing. When Allah (the Exalted) loves a servant, He gives him sincere excellent actions and successful belief that causes him to go to paradise. Or at the very least, He will give him

---

[20] Quran: al-Takwir 81:29.
[21] Quran: al-Ma'idah 5:38.

belief in Him that will make him have endless bliss.

The pleasure of Allah (the Exalted) is connected to sincere acts of worship. Allah (the Exalted) is pleased by people doing sincere acts of worship and people accepting Islam.

$$ لِيَقْضِيَ ٱللَّهُ أَمْراً كَانَ مَفْعُولاً $$

"Allah surely destined all matters and [they are already] done."[22] The emphasis that is present in this verse cannot fully be expressed in the English language. Whatever Allah has already done has already been decreed in all matters. Whatever He decrees has already been recorded and there is no change to it at all. So all our actions have all been decreed; as is all our provision and so on. The word *qada* (destiny) means knowing the limits of a thing and the time in which it will conclude. So our lifespans and death are already decreed.

$$ إِنَّ ٱللَّهَ عَلَىٰ كُلِّ شَيْءٍ قَدِيرٌ $$

"Allah truly has power of all things."[23] Allah (the Exalted) has power over all things and every living

---

[22] Quran: al-Tawbah 9:42.
[23] Quran: al-Baqarah 2:20.

thing is subject to His power. The decree of Allah (the Exalted) is only connected to the possible not the impossible. Allah (the Exalted) knows the impossible even though it does not exist. Note this is in terms of Islamic belief and needs explaining to one. Know that defects or blemishes are not part of the *dhat* (Essence) of Allah ever. Anyone who attributes errors or mistakes to Allah has disbelieved.

$$ ذَٰلِكُمُ ٱللَّهُ رَبُّكُمْ لَا إِلَٰهَ إِلَّا هُوَ خَٰلِقُ كُلِّ شَيْءٍ $$

"That is Allah, your Lord, there is no deity except Him, and He is the creator of everything."[24] Allah is the creator of everything, everything that is visible, invisible, known and unknown.

His ruling is His decision and what matters, and everything else is overruled. His knowledge is greater that anyone's and it is part of His wonderful name al-'Alim (the All-Knowledgeable).

$$ وَمَا تَوْفِيقِي إِلَّا بِٱللَّهِ $$

"I have no success except by Allah."[25] *Tawfiq* is a very difficult word to translate; "success" or

---

[24] Quran: al-An'am 6:102.

"divine enablements" are just two possibilities. It means that Allah has provided all the means for that thing to be. Imam al-Ghazali (may Allah show him mercy) said, "*Tawfiq* is when the desire of the servant matches the decree of Allah."

بَلْ هُوَ قُرْآنٌ مَّجِيدٌ فِي لَوْحٍ مَّحْفُوظٍ

"Rather it is the Majestic Quran in the Preserved Tablet."[26] Imam al-Maturidi (may Allah show him mercy) said that the Tablet (*Lawh*) contains every single command and everything that will exist forever. All the actions of mankind are present on it and many other things that have not happened.

---

[25] Quran: Hud 11:88.
[26] Quran: al-Buruj 85:21–2.

The virtuous

والفضيلة ليست بأمر الله تعالى ولكن بمشيئته
ومحبته ورضاه وقضائه وقدره وتخليقه
وكتابته في اللوح المحفوظ

"The virtuous is not the command of Allah, the Exalted, but it is by His will, His love, His pleasure, His predestination, His decree, His creating and it is recorded in the Preserved Tablet."

Commentary

As we said previously, the virtuous are extra *sunnah* and *nafl* actions. These actions increase one's reward and are not specific commands (*fard* or *wajib*) of Allah (the Exalted). It is better to do them but not sinful to leave them.

وَٱللَّهُ خَلَقَكُمْ وَمَا تَعْمَلُونَ

"Allah created you and what you do."[27] This verse serves as a refutation to the Mu'tazilite belief that

---

[27] Quran: al-Saffat 37:96.

the servant creates his own works. The correct belief is that Allah (the Exalted) created the action and the servant makes the choice. If there were no choice then there would be no basis for reward and punishment.

If a servant can make his own actions then is he doing an act of rebellion or doing something that Allah is not aware of? Of course, this argument is baseless. All our actions were created before we were ever born. This refutes the Mu'tazilite belief in this matter.

Abu Hanifah (may Allah show him mercy) was talking to a Mu'tazilite about this matter then asked him to make the sound *ha* from the place of *ba*. The Mu'tazilite was unable to do so because it is impossible.

Disobedience

والمعصية ليست بأمر الله ولكن بمشيئته لا
بمحبته وبقضائه لا برضاه وبتقديره لا بتوفيقه
وبخذلانه وعلمه وكتابته

"Disobedience is not the command of Allah, but it is in His will; not what He loves, it is in His predestination, not His good pleasure; it is in His decree, not His given success [*tawfiq*] but rather forsaking [His servant]; it is by His knowledge and it is recorded."

Commentary

Allah (the Exalted) has not commanded the person to commit sin. Rather, it is only through the servant believing the *nafs* (ego) and satan being overcome by his passions. There was a sect who were convinced that a servant is compelled to commit sin and this is major error. Anyone forced into sin cannot be judged over his sins because that is oppression. Allah (the Exalted) does not oppress His servants and therefore the servant has a choice.

إِن تَكْفُرُواْ فَإِنَّ اللَّهَ غَنِيٌّ عَنكُمْ وَلاَ يَرْضَى لِعِبَادِهِ الْكُفْرَ

"If you disbelieve, Allah has no need of you, He is not pleased with disbelief for His servants."[28] Imam al-Samarqandi (may Allah show him mercy) narrates that al-Kalabi said, "Allah is not pleased with disbelief for His servants as their religion." Allah does not love sin but the person has a choice, and this is why the action is created.

Being forsaken (khidlan) is when someone continues to commit sins and does this over a long period of time and thus becomes forsaken. This means that the door of repentance is not visible to his heart and he continues in his sin for years. This is the opposite of tawfiq. Being forsaken is when the avenues to sin are open to him. This is a punishment and what the following verse refers to:

فِي قُلُوبِهِم مَّرَضٌ فَزَادَهُمُ ٱللَّهُ مَرَضاً

"In their hearts is a disease; and so Allah increases the disease."[29] Imam al-Tabarani (may Allah show him mercy) said, "It means [He causes increase] in

[28] Quran: al-Zumar 39:7.
[29] Quran: al-Baqarah 2:10.

doubt and hypocrisy. Hypocrisy is called a disease because it destroys the person, for it is a disruption in his religion in regard to belief by the tongue [alone] and disbelief is by the heart. So his state is like the state of the sick, those who are caught between life and death."

The increase in disease is also an increase in sins because they would have to either repent in this world, or answer for all their sins on the Day of Judgement. In the context of the verse, the Quran is referring to those who profess belief merely on the tongue but have nothing in their hearts. Note that no action is mentioned here, but rather it is faith in the heart with affirmation on the tongue.

A person in a state of sin must repent, make wudu and pray two units of the Prayer of Repentance as reported by many Companions, including Abu Bakr and 'Ali (may Allah be pleased with them).

Allah knows all of your actions, what choice you made in depths of your heart and the choice that you let everyone know of. All of this is recorded on the Preserved Tablet and it cannot change. The Mother of the Book (Umm al-Kitab) changes nightly but not the Preserved Tablet. The Mother of the Book is the decree that is taken from the Preserved Tablet before it appears in this world.

This decree can change, and this is the decree which supplication can change, but not the Preserved Tablet.

Third point: Sunni interpretation

و[الثالث] نقر بأن الله سبحانه وتعالى على
العرش استوى من غير أن يكون له حاجة
واستقرار عليه

"[Third point:] Allah, Glorious and Exalted, inscribed that He established the Throne without being in need of it or to be affirmed by it."

Commentary

This was one of the second "problems" that manifest in the early community. Are certain verses to be taken literally or not?

There are four methods in addressing this question: (1) *ta'wil*, interpretation; (2) *tafwid*, submitting to the meaning; (3) *tashbih*, anthropomorphism, and *tajasum*, literalism; and (4) *ta'til*, rejection.

The first point is interpretation, which can be one of two ways. The first is Sunni interpretation and another is literally translating the verse. The Sunni interpretation is the way of the Ash'ari school and the Khalaf (fourth to fifth century of Islam), who translate a verse according to the majesty of Allah (the Exalted). The problem with translating something literally into another language means that the meaning is lost and it could cause delusion.

The second method is the way of the Maturidis and Hanafis, in which we do not interpret it but rather surrender the meaning to Allah (the Exalted). However, if we translate it then we use the Ash'ari method of interpretation above. This is the way of the true Salaf (first to third century).

The third method is used by the Mujassimun and modern-day Salafis and Wahhabis. They ignore the *ijma'* (scholarly consensus) on this issue and take the verses literally and make Allah into a human being with like body parts. This is part of their innovation and misguidance and anyone who involves themselves in these issues will be confused for decades.

The fourth method is also rejected, which is the rejection of these verses and this is also an error. We accept all the Quran but reject the interpretation of the ignorant. Rejection of a verse of the Quran is like rejecting it all and this is disbelief. We use the first two methods and reject the second two.

It is from the error of many translators to literally translate these verses and somehow claim it to be a Sunni translation! How can this be when it is often *tajsim* or anthropomorphism? A correct translation of the verse is as follows:

ٱلرَّحْمَـٰنُ عَلَى ٱلْعَرْشِ ٱسْتَوَىٰ

"The All-Merciful established the Throne."[30] This is a correct translation using the method of *ta'wil* taking into account His majesty. The Wahhabi translation of this verse contains many errors: "The Most Gracious (Allah) rose over (*istawa*) the (Mighty) Throne (in a manner that suits His Majesty)."[31] The Wahhabis have used direction and place as a description for Allah by making Him like His creation, which is rejected by the Quran itself. This translation also indicates that Allah was in need of the Throne, which is baseless. "Al-Rahman", moreover, is closer to the meaning of "All-Merciful" and further from the meaning of "Gracious".

If these are the errors present in one translated verse then imagine the errors in the complete

---

[30] Quran: TaHa 20:5.
[31] M. Taqi-ud-Din al-Hilali and M. Muhsin Khan, *Interpretation of the Meanings of the Noble Quran* (Darussalam, 2001), p. 621.

translation! This was never the way of the Salaf or Khalaf but the way of the anthropomorphists. The Wahhabis and selefis say that Allah sits on the Throne and this is rejected by the entirety of Ahl al-Sunnah wa al-Jama'ah, because they have made Allah into a man and this is rejected. Allah is beyond our understanding and therefore is not like human beings or anything created.

Imam Abu Mansur al-Maturidi (may Allah show him mercy) said, "To suggest a place for Allah is idolatry."[32]

Imam Zahid al-Kawthari (may Allah show him mercy) said, "'The Merciful established the throne': whoever denies that the Merciful established the Throne has denied a verse from the Glorious Dhikr [Quran] and thereby commits disbelief. However, the establishment (*istawa*) for Allah (the Exalted) is an *istiwa* that befits His majesty according to the meaning intended by Allah Most High and by the Messenger of Allah (may Allah bestow peace and blessings upon him), without prodding the meaning in accordance with the path of the Salaf such as Ibn Mahdi.

---

[32] Ibn Jahbal al-Kilabi, *The Refutation of Him Who Attributes Direction to Allah*, p. 16.

"The path of the Khalaf is to understand this to mean sovereignty (*mulk*) and the like, as dictated by language. In this, there is no negation of the verse. This can never be said of them! As for understanding it to mean 'sitting' and 'settlement', this is manifest deviance."[33] We can see that Imam al-Kawthari (may Allah show him mercy) is presenting the Maturidi position of the early community.

Imam Malik (may Allah show him mercy) said,

الإستواء معلوم والكيف مجهول والسؤال عنه بدعة والإيمان واجب

"*Al-Istiwa'* is known, the modality is unknown, asking about it is innovation and belief in it is necessary."[34] This is the real understanding of someone who was of the real Salaf, and was not a selefi – those who falsely claiming that they are born in a century that rejects them and whom we reject. There are four parts to the answer that Imam Malik presented: we know that there is *istiwa'*; we do not know how; we believe in the verse because

---

[33] Ibid., p. 126, an excellent translation by Sheikh Gibril Haddad.
[34] Mulla Ali al-Qari, *Daw' al-Ma'ali*, although this is also well reported.

it is part of the Quran; and it is blameworthy to ask about it.

The verb *istawa* is used often to mean "to have control", like *Qad istawa Bishr 'ala Iraq*, 'Bishr has full authority over Iraq.'[35] Hence the translation of the verse, "The All-Merciful established the Throne."

Do not be deluded into having an average Muslim understanding of these verses. Rather, they are all used in different contexts and removing them from those contexts means that you will be misguided.

---

[35] Ibid.

Allah does not need anything

وهو حافظ العرش وغير العرش من غير احتياج فلو كان محتاجا لما قدر على إيجاد العالم والحفظ وتدبيره كالمخلوقين ولو صار محتاجا إلى الجلوس والقرار فقبل خلق العرش أين كان الله تعالى؟ تعالى الله عن ذلك علوا كبيرا!!!!

"He maintains the Throne, and everything besides, without being in need. For if He were to be in need [of it], He would not possess the omnipotent power to bring into existence the world, preserve it and manage it, much like those who are created. If He were to be in need of 'sitting' or 'staying', where was Allah (the Exalted) before He created the Throne? Allah is free of having any need absolutely."

Commentary

Allah (the Exalted) created the Throne so how could He be in need of it? Just like Allah (the Exalted) created time and place and is not in need of them; moreover, Allah (the Exalted) is not in need of anything but we are the ones in need of Him. Allah (the Exalted) describes Himself as al-Ghani – "the one free of need" is its literal meaning – and Allah (the Exalted) has no needs because He is not like His creation. Created things have needs, like water, air, sleep and so on. Allah (the Exalted) created all these for everyone and therefore He is not in need of them.

The Prophet (may Allah bestow peace and blessings upon him) said,

كان الله ولم يكن شئ غيره

"Allah was, and there was nothing else besides."[36] There are other narrations that have the word "*ma'ahu*" (with him), while other words and other narrations add a long sentence to this but that part is not accepted. The additional part was from a commentary.

The part in which we all agree is that there was Allah (the Exalted) and nothing else existed.

Then when Allah (the Exalted) decreed that He would bring things into existence, He did.

---

[36] Bukhari and al-Hakim.

Therefore, He was never in need of anything before creation and is certainly not in need of anything now. If you understand this correctly then you have understood a great part of your religion.

Anyone who accuses Allah (the Exalted) of having human parts or resembling creation has made a grave and serious error.

Fourth point: The Quran is the speech of Allah

[والرابع] نقر بأن القرآن كلام الله تعالى غير
مخلوق ووحيه وتنزيله وصفته لا هو ولا غيره
بل هو صفته على التحقيق

"[Fourth point:] it is inscribed that the Quran is the uncreated speech of Allah (the Exalted), His divine inspiration, His revelation, as He described, but it is not Him nor another; rather, it is released as He described."

Commentary

The question of whether the Quran was created or not was one of the first causes for dissension in the Muslim community.

The conclusion was that the Quran is the speech of Allah (the Exalted) and anything that pertains to Him is not created. The Quran is protected on the Preserved Tablet and cannot be removed.

The word "*sifatuhu*" (as He described) is in some narrations of this text and not others. The Mu'tazilites reject this and say it is created. We reply by saying that the speech of Allah is not created; rather, it is His attribute and therefore not created.

Imam Ahmad (may Allah show him mercy) held the position that the Quran was uncreated and because of this the caliph jailed the Imam. He was then lashed and scourged to make him agree, but he refused to bend the truth. This lasted twenty-seven months but he did not budge.

The Quran was revealed to the Prophet (may Allah bestow peace and blessings upon him) either directly or via Jibril (upon him be peace) who brought the revelation.

The verses are mostly Makki or Madani, meaning either revealed in Makkah or Medinah, respectively, and a small number were revealed elsewhere.

Ibn Mas'ud (may Allah be pleased with him) said he knew where and when each verse was revealed. One can but wonder at the knowledge of the Companions about the Quran, so how about the knowledge of the Prophet (may Allah bestow peace and blessings upon him), which is wondrous!

Recorded

مكتوب في المصاحف مقروء بالألسن محفوظ
في الصدور غير حال فيها والحبر والكاغد
والكتابة كلها مخلوقة لأنها أفعال العباد

"[The Quran is] recorded in *mushaf*s, recited on tongues, memorised in hearts without being changed, while the ink, paper and writing [therein] are all created because they are the actions of the servant."

Commentary

The Quran is recorded and that is the recording of the servant and his action. These words cannot be bettered and whenever we read about the Quran, in terms of this issue, we find the same words in all the books of Sunni belief. Note that the Arabs call the recorded Quran a *mushaf*, meaning scrolls, and in other countries it is simply referred to as the Quran.

There is a difference between the speech of Allah (the Exalted) and the actions of the servant. These

73

are two separates things and should not be confused.

Understanding the recording

وكلام الله سبحانه وتعالى غير مخلوق لأن
الكتابة والحروف والكلمات والآيات كلها آلات
القرآن لحاجة العباد إليها وكلام الله تعالى قائم
بذاته ومعناه مفهوم بهذه الأشياء فمن قال بأن
القرآن مخلوق فهو كافر بالله العظيم والله
تعالى معبود لا يزال عما كان وكلامه مقروء
ومكتوب ومحفوظ من غير مزايلة عنه عن
الموصوف

"The speech of Allah, Glorious and Exalted, is uncreated because writing, letters, words and verses are all instruments of the Quran that the servant is need of [to understand it]. The speech of Allah (the Exalted) is established in His *dhat*, meaning understood through these things. Whoever says that the Quran is created is a disbeliever of Allah, the Greatest. Allah (the Exalted) is [deserving of our] worship and is now as He ever was. His speech is recited, recorded and protected without it being separated from Him whom it is an attribute of."

Commentary

This is a confirmation of the first lines of the fourth point and provides us more details. We say that the Quran is the speech of Allah and that it is uncreated. The actions of the servant to record the Quran are created and this is not to be confused with the Quran itself.

The heavenly books are the Quran, Torah, Injil, scrolls of Ibrahim and Musa and the books of Adam. The Quran is the only divine text that remains in its original language of revelation. The Quran was revealed gradually over the period of twenty-three years and this allowed the Companions to practise the Quran over a long period.

Dhat is the Arabic term for essence or being but these are not good translations, though essence is the better of the two.

The Quran will return to Allah (the Exalted) before the Day of Judgement because of the neglect and opposition of Muslims. It will be raised, or withdrawn, from this world slowly: first in recitation, then the meanings and finally will be raised in its entirety.

Fifth point: The ranks of the Companions

و[الخامس] نقر بأن أفضل هذه الأمة بعد
نبينا محمد صلى الله عليه وسلم أبو بكر
الصديق ثم عمر ثم عثمان ثم علي رضوان
الله عليهم أجمعين

"[Fifth point:] it is inscribed that the best of this nation after our Prophet Muhammad (may Allah bestow peace and blessings upon him) is Abu Bakr the Truthful, then 'Umar, then 'Uthman and then 'Ali (may Allah be pleased with them all)."

Commentary

Our Prophet Muhammad (may Allah bestow peace and blessings upon him) is the best creation of Allah (the Exalted). Allah (the Exalted) describes the Prophet (may Allah bestow peace and blessings upon him) as a mercy to all the worlds. The Prophet (may Allah bestow peace and blessings upon him) has been given the grand intercession and these two points are enough for us to understand the superiority of our Prophet (may Allah bestow peace and blessings upon him).

Imam Ahmad (may Allah show him mercy) said, "We believe that Muhammad (may Allah bestow peace and blessings upon him) is the best messenger, the final prophet and witness for all."[37]

Imam al-Nawawi (may Allah show him mercy) has a chapter on the superiority of our Prophet Muhammad (may Allah bestow peace and blessings upon him) over all creation in *Riyad al-Salihin*.

'Abd al-Ghani al-Maqdasi (may Allah show him mercy) said, "We believe that Muhammad, the Chosen, is the best of all creation, the most virtuous and most honoured by Allah, Glorious and Exalted, the highest in rank and the closest means to Allah."[38]

More can be read in Sheikh Yusuf al-Nabhani's *Muhammadan Bounties* (Sheikhy Notes, 2019).

We affirm that Abu Bakr is the best of this nation after the Prophet (may Allah bestow peace and blessings upon him) followed by 'Umar, 'Uthman

---

[37] *Tabaqat Hanbali*, 2/279.
[38] *'Aqidah al-Hafiz al-Maqdasi*, p. 52.

and then 'Ali (may Allah be pleased with them all). Getting into arguments about which Companion is better is not what people should do with their time. Rather, they should look at what they can learn about their lives to make their own lives better. I have published books on each of these four Companions and a general book on the virtues of the Companions, which is based on forty hadith that I have given commentary to, further expanding the points of their virtues. I prove that there was a lot of respect between the four caliphs and there is at least one hadith each to prove that fact. The companions who accepted Islam before the conquest of Mekkah are at a higher rank than those after. From the elite companions are those who were martyred before the conquest.

Abu Hanifah (may Allah show him mercy) uses the term *"ridwan Allah 'alayhim"*, meaning "may the pleasure of Allah be upon them". The *ridwan* of Allah is so great it cannot be manifest in this world and it is only manifest in paradise. We say that Allah (the Exalted) knows best about the disagreements between the Companions.

The way of Ahl al-Sunnah is to honour and respect all the companions and the Ahl al-Bayt. Being extreme to one side means one will leave Ahl al-Sunnah.

Respecting those who proceeded us

لقوله تعالى وَالسَّابِقُونَ السَّابِقُونَ أُولَئِكَ
الْمُقَرَّبُونَ فِي جَنَّاتِ النَّعِيمِ وكل من كان أسبق
فهو أفضل يحبهم كل مؤمن تقي ويبغضهم كل
منافق شقي

"The Exalted said, 'The out-strippers have proceeded; they are brought close; in the blessed paradise.'[39] Those who proceeded are more virtuous. Every fearful believer loves them and every wretched hypocrite hates them."

Commentary

The way of Ahl al-Sunnah is one of balance, in love of the Companions and Ahl al-Bayt, because some Companions are also part of the latter. Preferring one group over the other is to leave Ahl al-Sunnah. So we combine our love and respect for both groups because they are essentially one.

---

[39] Quran: al-Waqi'ah 56:10–12.

The Companions are those who testified to the truth of the message of the Prophet (may Allah bestow peace and blessings upon him) and died in a state of faith.

Those who outstripped others are those who proceeded with sincere acts of worship more than the others. Therefore, those who precede others do so because they are more virtuous and this is often related about the Companions.

Loving the Companions is a wonderful act and if you were to read their life stories then you would take great admonition from them. Cursing a Companion is a major sin but rejecting a Companion is disbelief, for it is rejection of something mass transmitted. Some scholars, because of their high regard for them, deem cursing a Companion to be disbelief, but this is not widely accepted.

Point six: The servant's actions

و[السادس] نقر بأن العبد مع أعماله وإقراره
ومعرفته مخلوق فلما كان الفاعل مخلوقا
فأفعاله أولى بأن تكون مخلوقة وأن الله تعالى
خلق الخلق

"[Point six:] it is inscribed that the servant along with his actions, affirmation and realisation are created. So when the doer is created then his actions are necessarily created. Allah (the Exalted) created all creation [and their actions]."

Commentary

In regard of the servant, all his actions are created by Allah (the Exalted). This includes his affirmation and realisation; this explains to us the great blessings of these works. Notice that realisation is part of affirmation here.

وَٱللَّهُ خَلَقَكُمْ وَمَا تَعْمَلُونَ

"Allah created you and what you do."[40] In the context of the verse it is in reference to Ibrahim (upon him be peace) but it applies to everyone. The usage of the plural *kum* negates the possibility that it is meant for only one person.

Allah (the Exalted) created everything and everyone and what they do, but mankind and jinn have a choice. Choice is the basis for reward or punishment. This is called *kasb*, as confirmed by Imam al-Qurtubi (may Allah show him mercy). *Kasb* is acquisition of the choices that one makes. Know that there are things within your choice and things outside. If a person becomes ill then this is normally not his choice but his acquisition is how he handles the illness.

Ibn 'Ajibah (may Allah show him mercy) said about this verse, "This is our proof that actions are created by Allah (the Exalted). Meaning that Allah created you all and created your actions, so why would you worship anyone besides?"

One of the Ahl al-Bayt said he is astonished that Allah created our actions but gives us the reward for them!

---

[40] Quran: al-Saffat 37:96.

Provision

ولم يكن لهم طاقة لأنهم ضعفاء عاجزون والله
تعالى خالقهم ورازقهم لقوله تعالى واللهُ الَّذِي
خَلَقَكُمْ ثُمَّ رَزَقَكُمْ ثُمَّ يُمِيتُكُمْ ثُمَّ يُحْيِيكُمْ

"They do not have the strength because they are weak and incapable. Allah, the Exalted, created them and gave them provision. The Exalted said, 'It is Allah who created you, then gave you provision, then caused you to die and then brought you back to life.'"

Commentary

Neither mankind nor jinn can benefit from themselves unless Allah (the Exalted) allows them to do so. Man can get sick and die from small aliments from unseen bacteria. Allah (the Exalted) created everything and then gives them all provision.

Imam al-Samarqandi (may Allah show him mercy) said,

ٱللَّهُ ٱلَّذِى خَلَقَكُمْ ولم تكونوا شيئاً ثُمَّ رَزَقَكُمْ
يعني: أطعمكم ما عشتم في الدنيا ثُمَّ يُمِيتُكُمْ عند
انقضاء آجالكم ثُمَّ يُحْيِيكُمْ للبعث بعد الموت
لينبئكم بما عملتم في الدنيا ويجازيكم

"'It is Allah who created you' when you were
nothing, 'then gave you provision', meaning with
that which nourishes you in the world, 'then
caused you to die' when your lifetimes come to an
end, 'then brought you back to life' to be
resurrected after death to be informed about what
you did in the world and to be recompensed."

This verse confirms the point that Allah (the
Exalted) created us and gave us provision so we
can maintain our bodies. We die and go to the
grave and then are resurrected on the Day of
Judgement. Then we are recompensed for the
choices we made in the world. Recompensed can
mean either for the good or evil that we did.

Halal and haram provision

والكسب حلال وجمع المال من الحلال حلال
وجمع المال من الحرام حرام

"Acquisition is lawful and gathering wealth from lawful means is lawful, while gathering wealth that is unlawful is unlawful."

Commentary

Halal is different in everything that it applies to. In terms of food, it refers to meat from a slaughtered animal, and does not contain pork or alcohol/wine.

In terms of clothes, it is something that covers the nakedness of someone, which differs for men and women.

In terms of work, it is a job that has no oppression, no interest (usury) and nothing linked with any sin like transporting haram substances: wine/alcohol, pork, blood, drugs and so forth.

Provision (*rizq*) is whatever we use in this world and not what we merely possess because that is not *rizq*. Haram in money is anything that involves usury, oppression, drugs, murder, theft, lies, wine/alcohol and pork.

Gathering wealth that is lawful is lawful although it is better to spend some in charity after one has paid their zakat.

Gathering wealth that is unlawful is unlawful and none of it benefits anyone. Even if one were to earn money via wine/alcohol, drugs or interest then it would have no benefit, not even if spent in charity. One of the Salaf said that giving charity with unlawful wealth is like trying to clean one's clothes with urine! The clothes are not going to get clean and if anything they will smell even more!

In terms of provision, the Mu'tazilites disagree that something haram is provision. The haram part is the acquisition of the slave in attaining the wealth and not the provision itself.

Know that the halal and haram do not apply to Allah (the Exalted); rather, they only apply to creation. There is section in the fiqh books called *Khatar wa Ibahah* that needs to studied by all.

Seventh point: Three types of people

[وَالسابع] وَالناس عَلى ثلاثة أصناف المؤمن المخلص في إيمانه وَالكافر الجاحد في كفره وَالمنافق الدامس في نفاقه

"[Point seven:] people are of three types: the sincere believer in his faith, the rejecting disbeliever in his disbelief and the concealed hypocrite in his hypocrisy."

Commentary

وَقُلِ ٱلْحَقُّ مِن رَّبِّكُمْ فَمَن شَآءَ فَلْيُؤْمِن وَمَن شَآءَ فَلْيَكْفُرْ إِنَّا أَعْتَدْنَا لِلظَّالِمِينَ نَاراً أَحَاطَ بِهِمْ

"Say: the Truth is from your Lord, whoever wills to believe should do so and whoever wills to disbelieve [should do so]; We have prepared for disbelievers a great [and overwhelming] fire that totally encompasses them."[41] This verse explains

---

[41] Quran: al-Kahf 18:29.

to us that belief is not forced but rather it is the choice of the individual, and there is a warning that if someone disbelieves, their final abode is hell. Hell is indefinite here, meaning that there are many different types of fire in it and there is no way out and this is what "encompassing" means. The fire is so large and so engulfing and so terrifying that there is no escape from the eternal torment.

Imam al-Samarqandi (may Allah show him mercy) said, "Whoever wishes to believe should say the Testimony of Faith: there is no deity except Allah …"

Imam Abu Hanifah (may Allah show him mercy) said that there are three types of people and they have different obligations based on their situation.

The sincere believer in his faith is the one who has a strong conviction that Islam is the truth. His actions might not be valid or he fails continuously. Yet his belief is present and he could detest his sins and feels weak to clean up his life. But his faith remains no matter what happens in his life. The work of the sincere believer is to maintain his obligations and even though he might fail, it is his work that his focus is on. He should believe correctly and this is also part of his obligations.

The disbeliever feels safe in his disbelief and his worldview is shaped in this rejection. He feels that religion has chained him and that he has removed this chain. However, when we look at the verse we are reminded that rejection in this life has consequences in the next. The consequence is that hell is awaiting them. There is a place already prepared for a disbeliever in hell and a place already prepared for the believer in paradise.

The concealed hypocrite is he who manifests faith on his tongue without there being faith in the heart. He thinks what he is doing is correct and this delusion means that he is going to hell as well. In this world, we can pretend to be people who we are not but in the other world, we cannot pretend. Everything shall be made clear and known, whether we like it or not.

The responsibility of each of them

وَاللهُ تعالى فرض على المؤمن العمل وعلى الكافر الإيمان وعلى المنافق الإخلاص لقوله تعالى يَٰٓأَيُّهَا ٱلنَّاسُ ٱتَّقُوا رَبَّكُمْ يعني أيها المؤمنون أطيعوا وأيها كافرون آمنوا وأيها المنافقون أخلصوا

"Allah, the Exalted, has made actions obligatory for the believer, faith an obligation for the disbeliever and sincerity an obligation for the hypocrite. As the Exalted said, 'O people, fear your Lord,'[42] meaning: 'O believers, obey', 'O disbelievers, believe' and 'O hypocrites, be sincere'."

Commentary

Here we can see the great knowledge of Imam Abu Hanifah (may Allah show him mercy) in how he explains one verse and applies it to all people, in particular the three kinds he mentions. The

---

[42] Quran: al-Nisa' 4:1.

obligations are different for each set of people. "O people, fear your Lord" – how is this fear actualised? The word *tawqa* is mentioned in the verse, whose root meaning is to parry a blow. If someone was about to strike you then you would block the strike with your hands. This fear means different things to different people.

The believer actualises fear by doing the obligations and refraining from sins as much as he is able. If he commits sins then he repents immediately and does not return to them.

The disbeliever's only obligation is to believe. So he should look at his faith and find faith in Islam and become Muslim. A disbeliever has no obligations in Islam at all and nor should we make disbelievers accept Islamic rulings. This is tantamount to oppression and we should not oppress anyone.

The hypocrite should be sincere by founding his faith on certainty. Removing doubts from his heart by finding answers, instead of shouting and screaming in gatherings to make himself look good. The previous religions only prescribed sincerity and a Muslim needs sincerity too. The sincerity for other nations was concerning their actions not faith. The hypocrite here must make his faith sincerity in his heart by basing it on truthfulness.

We all have work to be getting on with and these are our duties.

Eighth point: Ability

[وَالثامن] نقر بأن الاستطاعة مع الفعل لا قبل الفعل ولا بعد الفعل لأنه لو كان قبل الفعل لكان العبد مستغنيا عن الله تعالى وقت الحاجة فهذه خلاف حكم النص لقوله تعالى وَاللهُ الْغَنِيُّ وَأَنْتُمُ الْفُقَرَاءُ ولو كان بعد الفعل لكان من المحال لأنه حصول الفعل بلا استطاعة

"[Point eight]: it is inscribed that ability is conjoined with action, not before or after it. For if it were before action then the servant would be free from Allah, the Exalted, in the time of need, and this contradicts the ruling of the text of the Exalted, 'Allah is free of need and it is you who are impoverished.'[43] If it were after the action then it would be impossible because it would necessitate the occurrence of the action without ability and strength."

Commentary

---

[43] Quran: Muhammad 47:38.

Istita'ah means ability and its root word *ta'ah* means obedience, which gives us an indication that our ability should be used for acts of obedience. The ability to do the action comes at the time the action is done not before or after it.

A sect called the *Jabariyyah* believed that everything was forced on the servant and that he had no choice. This is refuted because without choice there is no point to reward and punishment. Imam Abu Hanifah (may Allah be pleased with him) refutes this an invalid idea.

If the ability is before the action then this again means someone can compel Allah (the Exalted) to accept their action, which is baseless. If it came after the ability then it would be impossible for someone to do something without ability and strength.

أبي موسى الأشعري رضي الله عنه أن رسول الله صلى الله عليه وسلم قال له: يَا عَبْدَ اللَّهِ بْنَ قَيْسٍ، قُلْت: لَبَّيْكَ يَا رَسُولَ اللَّهِ قال: أَلاَ أَدُلُّكَ عَلَى كَلِمَةٍ مِنْ كَنْزٍ مِنْ كُنُوزِ الْجَنَّةِ؟ قُلت: بَلَى، يَا رَسُولَ اللَّهِ فَدَاكَ أَبِي وَأُمِّي قَالَ: لاَ حَوْلَ وَلاَ قُوَّةَ إِلاَّ بِاللَّهِ

"Abu Musa al-Ash'ari (may Allah be pleased with him) reports that the Messenger of Allah (may Allah bestow peace and blessings upon him) said, 'O 'Abdullah ibn Qays.' He replied, 'At your disposal, O Messenger of Allah.' He said, 'Shall I not tell you about one of the treasures of paradise?' He said, 'Indeed do, O Messenger of Allah, may my parents be your ransom.' He said, 'There is no might or power except by Allah.'" Related by Muslim and Bukhari.

This hadith has many benefits and one is the good manners of the Companion, who was ready to do anything. This is a good lesson for any student with his teacher. *Labbayk* (at your disposal) is a phrase you would say to show respect and honour to someone. It is perhaps because of this respect that the Companion received a gift from paradise in the form of these words. *Hawl* means to change something, while power (*quwwah*) is like ability and linked to strength. The letter *ba'* with the name of Allah (the Exalted) means that unless He moves or puts the ability or power in something then it does not move or alter. However, the choice is still ours to make.

Point nine: Wiping leather socks

[والتاسع] نقر بأن المسح على الخفين واجب
للمقيم يوما وليلة وللمسافر ثلاثة أيام وليالي لأن
الحديث ورد هكذا فمن أنكر فإنه يخشى عليه
الكفر لأنه قريب من الخبر المتواتر

"[Point nine:] it is inscribed that wiping on leather socks is necessary [permitted] for twenty-four hours for every person, and three days for a traveller, in view of the [many] hadiths that are reported thus. Therefore, if anyone denies this, it is feared that they are a disbeliever, because it is close to being a mass-transmitted report."

Commentary

Hasan al-Basri (may Allah be pleased with him) said, "Seventy men of the Companions of the Messenger of Allah (may Allah bestow peace and blessings upon him) saw him wipe over leather socks."[44] For something to be mass transmitted it needs an undeniable number like the number mentioned here. Some scholars have different narrations of hadith, so some say that between four

---

[44] Imam al-Mawsili, *al-Ikhtiyar li-Ta'lil al-Mukhtar*, 1/28.

and seven onwards are considered mass transmission (*mutawatir*). However, for something to be mass transmitted, then, it needs to have a number that removes doubt about it completely, like seventy Companions. Leather socks are not very well known so it might be the reason that disbelief is feared for the rejecter of them.

'Ali ibn Abi Talib (may Allah be pleased with him) narrates that the Prophet (may Allah bestow peace and blessings upon him) said, "A traveller wipes for three days and nights, and a resident wipes for a day and night."[45]

So what Abu Hanifah (may Allah show him mercy) is saying here is based purely on the aforementioned hadith. He also says *wajib* (necessary) but it is actually *sunnah* to use leather socks and not *wajib*.

Other socks that are practically waterproof can be used, such as waterproof socks, because leather socks are essentially waterproof except the zip area. Thick mountain socks or water-resistant socks are not a valid substitute in the Hanafi *madhhab*.

---

[45] Muslim 286.

There is a very slight difference between the Shia and the Sunnis. The Shia believe that the bare top of the foot or normal socks can be wiped. This is not correct and renders one's wudu, as well as any action done with it like prayer or reading the Quran, invalid.

They feared disbelief because it was a rare action that not many people were aware of. So, for this reason, disbelief is feared for an individual and it is also not a disputed matter of belief but mass transmitted, so beware.

Shortening prayers

وَالقصرُ والإِفطارُ فِي السفرِ رخصة بنص
الكتابِ لِقولِهِ تعالى وَإِذَا ضَرَبْتُمْ فِي الأَرْضِ
فَلَيْسَ عَلَيْكُمْ جُنَاحٌ أَنْ تَقْصُرُوا مِنَ الصَّلَاةِ وفي
الإِفطارِ قولِهِ تعالى وَفَمَنْ كَانَ مِنْكُمْ مَرِيضاً أَوْ
عَلَى سَفَرٍ فَعِدَّةٌ مِنْ أَيَّامٍ أُخَرَ

"Shortening prayers and not fasting when travelling are dispensations according to the text of the Quran, in view of the Exalted having said, 'If you strike out in the earth then there is no crime to shorten your prayer.'[46] Regarding not fasting, the Exalted has said, 'Whoever of you is ill or travelling then make up the fasts on other days.'"[47]

Commentary

Qasr is the shortening of any obligatory four-*rak'ah* prayer to two units. Namely, you can shorten the obligatory units of *zuhr*, *'asr* and *'isha* to two units. The *sunnah* prayers can be left out

---

[46] Quran: al-Nisa' 4:101.
[47] Quran: al-Baqarah 2:184.

when travelling until when one arrives at their temporary station like a hotel and then from there can read them. The other two *fard* prayers (i.e. *fajr* and *maghrib*) are not shortened and nor any of the *sunnah* prayers. The meaning of "strike out in the earth", according to Imam al-Samarqandi (may Allah show him mercy), is to travel in the earth. The distance that constitutes "travel" here is eighty kilometres, and one can shorten once they leave their city and their total journey is eighty kilometres or over.

A person who is travelling or ill has an excuse not to fast, although if one can fast and travel, this is better but the person can choose not to fast, especially when it is difficult to find food. He has to set off travelling before the time of the fast enters or else he will have to fast that day.

The person who is ill can refrain from fasting until they are better, especially when fasting will increase or prolong their sickness. There are more details about fasting and prayer found in the books of fiqh. The above is according to the Hanafi *madhhab* so please refer to your own school. I am not aware if there was a difference between Sunnis and other sects at the time on this issue.

This could have been mentioned because there were sects outside the four *madhhab*s that do not adhere to this. So some groups shorten according to their whims and fast or break according to their whims.

Tenth point: The pen

[العاشر] نقر بأن الله تعالى أمر القلم بأن يكتب
فقال القلم ماذا أكتب يا رب فقال الله تعالى
أكتب ما هو كائن إلى يوم القيامة لقوله تعالى
وَكُلُّ شَيْءٍ فَعَلُوهُ فِي الزُّبُرِ وَكُلُّ صَغِيرٍ وَكَبِيرٍ
مُسْتَطَرٌ

"[Point ten:] it is inscribed that Allah, the Exalted, ordered the pen to write and it asked, 'What do I write, O Lord?' Allah, the Exalted, said, 'Write what will be until the Day of Judgement,'[48] in view of the Exalted having said, 'Everything they did is in the scriptures; every small and great thing is recorded.'"[49]

Commentary

There is another narration of the above hadith:

---

[48] Abu Dawud 4800; al-Tirmidhi 2155; Ahmad 5/317; al-Taylasi.
[49] Quran: 54:52–3.

إن أول ما خلق الله القلم. قال له: اكتب، فقال: يا رب وما أكتب؟ قال: اكتب مقادير كل شيء حتى تقوم الساعة. وفي لفظ: لما خلق الله القلم قال له: اكتب، فجرى بما هو كائن إلى قيام الساعة. رواه الطبراني

The Prophet (may Allah bestow and blessings upon him) said, "The first of the creation of Allah was the pen. Allah said to the pen, 'Write,' and it asked, 'What do I write, O Lord?' He said, 'Write the exact decree of everything until the Day of Judgement.'" In another narration, "When Allah created the pen, He said to it, 'Write what will occur until the end of time.'"[50]

There are many lessons to be learnt from this hadith. The decree for everyone has already been recorded and nothing will change and so there is nothing to fear. Know that whatever happens in the world is part of the decree of Allah (the Exalted) and if something evil occurs then know that the Day of Judgement is a terrible day for the oppressors. All of this is recorded on the Preserved Tablet and it cannot be changed.

---

[50] Al-Tabarani.

This is also the meaning of the surahs too, that everything is recorded in the Tablet. This does not mean that we do not try, for we have been put in the world to be tried and tested, but the final outcome is what Allah (the Exalted) has already decreed.

Qiyam al-sa'ah means the Day of Judgement but it refers to mostly standing because we will be made to wait to be judged. *Taqum al-sa'ah* means when the Hour arrives. *Sa'ah* in Modern Arabic means an hour, but the Day of Judgement is longer than that.

Eleventh point: Punishment of the grave

[و الحادي عشر] نقر بأن عذاب القبر كائن لا
محالة وسؤال منكر ونكير حق لورود
الأحاديث

"[Point eleven:] the punishment of the grave certainly occurs. The questioning of *Munkar* and *Nakir* is true because of the many reports."

Commentary

Imam Abu Hanifah (may Allah show him mercy) was the first to mention punishment of the grave in his works as an act of belief. It is mentioned in every book of Sunni Islamic belief since.

ٱلنَّارُ يُعْرَضُونَ عَلَيْهَا غُدُوّاً وَعَشِيّاً وَيَوْمَ تَقُومُ
ٱلسَّاعَةُ أَدْخِلُوٓا۟ آلَ فِرْعَوْنَ أَشَدَّ ٱلْعَذَابِ

"The fire is shown to them in the morning and evening, and when the Hour is established they will join the people of Pharaoh in the most severe torment."[51]

Imam Abu Layth al-Samarqandi (may Allah show him mercy) said,

اَلنَّارُ يُعْرَضُونَ عَلَيْهَا قال ابن عباس يعني تعرض أرواحهم على النار غُدُوّاً وَعَشِيّاً هكذا قال قتادة ومجاهد، وقال مقاتل: تعرض روح كل كافر على منازلهم من النار كل يوم مرتين

"'The fire is shown to them' – Ibn 'Abbas said it means their souls are shown the fire 'morning and evening'; Qatadah and Mujahid thus agree. Muqatil said, 'The soul of every disbeliever is shown its places in the fire, twice daily.'"

Punishment of the grave is a point that is disagreed over, and this one verse proves its reality beyond any doubt, because it is clear evidence from the Quran itself. What is conversely understood (mafhum al-mukhalifah) therefore is that the righteous souls will be shown paradise twice a day.

The following people are not punished in their graves: prophets and messengers, the awliya, martyrs and reciters of Surah Mulk (daily). I have written two articles that are for further reading: one

---

51 Quran: Ghafir 40:46.

on Surah Mulk and another on benefiting the deceased and punishment in the grave. Both provide us with more detail about these summarised points. Some groups deny the punishment of the grave.

The angels of the grave who come to punish one are called: *Munkar, Mankur* and *Nakir*. According to *Perfection of Faith* by 'Abd al-Haqq al-Dahlawi (may Allah show him mercy) there are two angels who give glad tidings: *Bashir* and *Mubashir*. The names *Munkar, Mankur* and *Nakir* indicates that we will deny the past and present sins greatly. The root word of all their names is to deny or reject.

The best way to avoid punishment in the grave is to make sure no one has a right that you have not fulfilled, that you have settled monetary accounts with everyone, that you have asked forgiveness for those whom you have wronged and so on. However, the most important of all matters is to die with Islam as one's faith.

The grave shows us where we are going. Those going to paradise will experience a breeze from paradise and those going to hell will smell the stench of hell and will have snakes who will bite them.

The punishment is felt by the body and the soul but another person will not be able to tell, just like you cannot tell where a sleeping person goes in their dreams, and how their experience of time is different than yours.

Paradise and hell

والجنة والنار حق مخلوقتان لأهلهما لقوله
تعالى في حق المؤمنين أَعِدَّتْ لِلْمُتَّقِينَ وفي حق
الكفرة أَعِدَّتْ لِلْكَافِرِينَ خلقهما الله تعالى للثواب
والعقاب

"Paradise and hell are true and created for those who belong in either of them, in view of the Exalted having said in regard to the believers, 'prepared for the pious,'[52] and concerning the disbelievers, 'prepared for the disbelievers'.[53] Allah has created them for reward and punishment."

Commentary

Some philosophers rejected that heaven and hell exist and fabricated lies about this matter. Their rejection is about whether they are created now, which they are, and the Quran proves as much. The Imam refutes them even before they arrived

---

[52] Quran: Aal 'Imran 3:133.
[53] Quran: al-Baqarah 2:24.

113

on the scene! The philosophers were influenced by Greek and other texts about scepticism and rationalists. Imam al-Ghazali (may Allah show him mercy) refuted them and brought belief back to its Islamic roots, by removing what was alien to it. Though this was mainly in the Islamic heartlands of Syria, Egypt and so on. The Maturidis and Hanafis always had a strong following in Bukhara and these regions.

The word *u'iddat* (prepared) means that paradise and hell are ready for their inhabitants, and currently exist and await them.

We know that paradise and hell exist by the text of the Quran but we are unaware of the location of either realm. You can read *What No Eye Has Seen* by Sheikh Muhammad ibn 'Alawi al-Maliki (may Allah show him mercy) (Sheikhy Notes, 2017), which explains all about paradise.

The fires of hell are also ready for the liars, the criminals, the disbelievers, the tyrants and so forth. This is a point that the Mu'tazilites also rejected and this verse shows that hell is ready.

Hell is a blessing for those who seek to avoid it by their faith, and is only a punishment for those without faith. If it were not for hell, we would not strive to be free from it. Paradise is the reward of the believers and hell is the punishment for the disbelievers.

The scales

وَالميزان حق لقوله تعالى وَنَضَعُ المَوَازِينَ
الْقِسْطَ لِيَوْم الْقِيَامَةِ وقراءة الكتب حق لقوله
تعالى اقْرَأْ كِتَابَكَ كَفَى بِنَفْسِكَ الْيَوْمَ عَلَيْكَ حَسِيباً

"The scales are true in view of the Exalted having said, 'We placed justice on the balances on the Day of Judgement.'[54] The reading of the books is true in view of the Exalted having said, 'Read your book and that is a sufficient reckoner.'"[55]

Commentary

The scales are what our good and evil deeds will be weighted on and they will be a confirmation of our final destination. However, as soon as we have entered the grave we will know where we will go. The scales are where we will have confirmation of which side is the weightier: the good or the evil. If the scales are even, then the intercession of the Prophet (may Allah bestow peace and blessings

---

[54] Quran: al-Anbiya' 21:47.
[55] Quran: al-Isra' 17:14.

upon him) will come and add more into the scales of goodness. Ibn 'Abbas (may Allah be pleased with him) said they are like two scales. Imam al-Samarqandi (may Allah show him mercy) said that good actions will come in a beautiful form and ugly actions will come in an ugly form.

The reading of the books is the reading of the books of one's deeds: the good and evil of it. Al-Hasan (may Allah show him mercy) said it is the same if one be literate or illiterate. There used to be a British television show called *This Is Your Life*, which celebrities would be invited to, and be shown their lives from childhood to adulthood. Then they would be presented with a book that recorded it all. But the book we will get on the Day of Judgement will have every single thing in it.

Hasib (reckoner) has the meaning, according to the Quranic commentators, of witness. If a person is good, they will get the book in their right hand; if evil then in their left; and if a tyrant then from behind. Every small deed is recorded including things we have forgotten all about. Be they evil or good, they are all recorded and nothing is left out. This is a record that we cannot argue or refuse. We may refuse our sins and reject the idea that we have done nothing wrong here in this world;

however, in the next world we have cannot refuse anything.

Twelfth point: Resurrection after death

[وَالثَّانِي عشر] نقر بأن الله تعالى يحيي هذا
النفوس بعد الموت ويبعثهم في يوم كان مقداره
خمسين ألف سنة للجزاء والثواب وأداء الحقوق
لقوله تعالى وَأَنَّ اللهَ يَبْعَثُ مَنْ فِي الْقُبُورِ

"[Point twelve:] it is inscribed that Allah, the Exalted, will bring the souls back to life after death. They shall all be resurrected on a day that is 50,000 years long – for reward, recompense and the restoral of rights – in view of the Exalted having said, 'Allah will resurrect whoever was in their graves.'"[56]

Commentary

The resurrection is part of the hadith of Jibril: the Prophet (may Allah bestow peace and blessings upon him) said,

---

[56] Quran: al-Hajj 22:7.

أن تُؤمِنَ باللهِ وملائِكَتِهِ وَكُتُبِهِ ورُسُلِهِ واليوم
الآخر وتُؤمِنَ بالقَدَرِ خَيرِهِ وَشرِّهِ

"[Faith] is to believe in Allah, His angels, His books, His messengers, the Last Day and to believe in divine decree, the good and the evil of it."[57]

This is called the Day of Judgement, the Day of the Religion, the Last Day, the Day of Resurrection, the Day of Reckoning and so forth. The many names of something uncover layers of meaning and highlight the importance of it. The hadith of Jibril contains all the major matters of Islamic belief that we all have to belief in, and rejecting them could entail disbelief, dependant on certain conditions.

This day is 50,000 years long according to our reckoning where we will be resurrected naked, the sun will be brought overhead and we will sweat according to our sins. Some to their ankles, some to their knees, to their waists and some will be drowning in their sweat.

The Quranic verse 70:4 explains where 50,000 years is referenced. Everyone shall be resurrected,

---

[57] Muslim and Imam Ahmad.

including those whose bodies were consumed by large animals, lost at sea and those who were not buried for whatever reason.

The resurrection is in the body and soul together. Some philosophers rejected one and accepted the other. I think that some of these points are a miracle of Abu Hanifah (may Allah show him mercy). It could be that these issues where relevant in his time and are relevant now.

The blessed meeting

ولقاء الله لأهل الجنة حق بلا بلا كيفية ولا تشبيه
ولا جهة

"It is true that Allah will meet the people of paradise; without modality, anthropomorphism and direction."

Commentary

وُجُوهٌ يَوْمَئِذٍ نَّاضِرَةٌ إِلَىٰ رَبِّهَا
نَاظِرَةٌ

"That day will faces be resplendent; gazing towards their Lord."[58] This is solely for the residents of paradise, and those in hell will never see Him. This is the greatest blessing of paradise, greater than all it pleasures. We do not assign direction or know how He will be seen but He will be seen. Those who are blessed to see him will have a further blessing of prostration in this time

---

[58] Quran: al-Qiyamah 75:22–3.

but others will be prevented from prostration. When people in paradise see Allah they will want to prostate, some will be allowed and some unable. Both groups are from the residents of paradise.

Anthropomorphism is what the Wahhabis and Mujassimun have fallen into, which is imagining Allah (the Exalted) to have human characteristics. This is refuted by the Quran itself:

$$لَيْسَ كَمِثْلِهِ شَيْءٌ وَهُوَ ٱلسَّمِيعُ ٱلْبَصِيرُ$$

"There is nothing similar to Him and He is the All-Hearing and All-Seeing."[59] If we understand this verse then we understand what Allah is and what He is not. He is not human and does not have anything that resembles a human being. The verses that mention body parts are metaphorical or the meaning is unknown to us and are not to be taken literally. Submitting the meaning to Allah (the Exalted) is the best method of the true Salaf and not modern selefis.

Know that whoever loves to meet Allah, Allah (the Exalted) loves to meet him. Whoever hates to meet Allah, Allah (the Exalted) hates to meet him. The

---

[59] Quran: al-Shura 42:11.

first are true believers and the second are
disbelievers.

Intercession

وشفاعة نبينا محمد صلى الله عليه وسلم حق لكل من هو من أهل الجنة وإن كان صاحب كبيرة

"The intercession of our Prophet Muhammad (may Allah bestow peace and blessings upon him) is true for everyone who is from the residents of paradise, even if they committed enormities."

Commentary

The deniers of the intercession are the Mu'tazilites and their ilk.

مَن ذَا ٱلَّذِي يَشْفَعُ عِنْدَهُ إِلاَّ بِإِذْنِهِ

"Who can intercede without His permission?"[60] This is a proof that it is possible and the forty or so hadith on this matter further attests to this claim. There are six types of intercession of the Prophet (may Allah bestow peace and blessings upon him):

---

[60] Quran: al-Baqarah 2:255.

(1) the grand intercession that will bring everyone to be judged after waiting for years; (2) entering some into paradise without reckoning; (3) saving the Muslims from the fire by reducing their time in it; (4) supplicating for Muslims who should remain in hell to be saved; (5) increasing the level of those in paradise: (6) saving people at the scales when their actions are weighted.

Those that can intercede are the prophets and messengers, the Companions, the *awliya*, the scholars, the truthful, the martyrs, those of good actions and so on.

The hadith about the Prophet (may Allah bestow peace and blessings upon him) interceding for those who have committed enormities is about those who died without repenting from them. It is hoped that one is forgiven when they repent from such sins, *in sha' Allah*. Those who have committed major sins are still Muslims as long as they do not think their sin is lawful or halal.

The way to attain to intercession is to visit the blessed grave of the Prophet (may Allah bestow peace and blessings upon him).

The disbelievers shall have no help nor any intercessor to assist them on the Day of Judgement.

The Quraysh worshipped idols in error, thinking that they would intercede with Allah, but intercession is different to this. Intercession is when one worships Allah (the Exalted) and hopes that because he is Muslim that he will get the intercession of the Prophet (may Allah bestow peace and blessings upon him). Along these lines are the practices of *tawassul* and *istighathah*, whereby we invoke Allah (the Exalted) to answer our prayers by mentioning those He has blessed.

The rank of the female Companions

وعائشة رضي الله عنها بعد خديجة الكبرى أفضل نساء العالمين وأم المؤمنين ومطهرة من الزنا برية عما قالت الروافض فمن شهد عليها بالزنا فهو ولد الزنا

"Aishah, after Khadijah al-Kubra (may Allah be pleased with them both), is the most virtuous of women in the universe, one of the Mothers of the Believers, pure from [the accusation of] fornication as [wrongly] claimed by the Rawafid; whoever claims to witness that she did so is themselves a child born out of wedlock!"

Commentary

The superiority of the female Companions is much debated. Aishah, Khadijah and Fatimah (may Allah be pleased with them) are from the elite, and Allah knows better their ranks.

It is reported in Muslim and Bukhari that the Prophet (may Allah bestow peace and blessings upon him) said,

كمل من رجال كثير ولم يكمل من النساء إلا
أربع مريم بنت عمران وآسية امرأة فرعون
وخديجة بنت خويلد وفاطمة بنت محمد وفضل
عائشة على النساء كفضل الثريد على سائر
الطعام

"Many men have been perfected, while none of the women have been perfected except four: Maryam, daughter of 'Imran; Asiya, wife of Pharaoh; Khadijah, daughter of Khuwaylid; Fatimah, daughter of Muhammad. The virtue of Aishah over women is like the virtue of *tharid* over all food."

Tharid is a mixed broth of meat, and meat is referred to the best dish because it was often expensive and rarely eaten. In living memory, meat was consumed once a week and now it is eaten twice a day or even more. The over-consumption of meat is not good for one's health. It is from this hadith that we find the word *kamil*, which has subsequently been used to describe spiritual masters. However, this is in terms of perfecting their character and not in terms of anything remotely divine.

Maryam was the mother of 'Isa (Jesus) (upon him be peace) and a chaste woman who was a *waliyyah*, though not a prophet. She was locked in a place of worship by her uncle Zakariyya (upon him be peace), for her safety, and he would return and find fruits with her – fruits which were out of season and so Zakariyya (upon him be peace) would be astonished at this.

Asiya was the wife of Pharaoh and when he found out that she had accepted Allah (the Exalted) as her Lord, the Pharaoh brutally tortured her until she died of her wounds.

Khadijah (may Allah show her mercy) was the first wife of the Prophet (may Allah bestow peace and blessings upon him). She was a businesswoman and recognised the wondrous nature of the Prophet (may Allah bestow peace and blessings upon him) and wanted to marry him. This blessed union brought forth all the children of the Prophet (may Allah bestow peace and blessings upon him) except one. She gave all her wealth for the service of the religion. She suffered greatly at the advent of the boycott and it goes without saying the year in which she died is called the Year of Sadness. The Prophet (may Allah bestow peace and blessings upon him) would remember her with affection for many years. Ibn Khaldun said her acceptance of Islam was a sign of prophethood because the Prophet (may Allah bestow peace and blessings upon him) offered Islam to everyone and they all thought about it for a time. Khadijah (may Allah show her mercy), however, did not hesitate or need time to think – she accepted it straight away and she is the first Muslim.

Fatimah (may Allah be pleased with her) is the blessed daughter of the Prophet (may Allah bestow peace and blessings upon him). It is from her to marriage with 'Ali ibn Abi Talib (may Allah be pleased with them) that the Ahl al-Bayt come from, mostly. She looked after the home and her children and had a noble rank.

The Messenger of Allah (may Allah bestow peace and blessings upon him) said,

فَاطِمَةُ بَضْعَةٌ مِنِّي فَمَنْ أَغْضَبَهَا أَغْضَبَنِي

"Fatimah is a part of me: whatever angers her, angers me."[61] This hadith is sufficient proof for some to say Fatimah (may Allah be pleased with her) is better because they said we cannot prefer anyone over a part of the Prophet (may Allah bestow peace and blessings upon him).

---

[61] Muslim and Bukhari.

She is a master of the women in paradise and when she enters paradise everyone will be commanded to lower their gaze until she enters it.

She was chaste and keep her honour in the world and this is her reward in the afterlife.

Please note there are many hadiths about the virtues of Fatimah (may Allah be pleased with her) and they can be found in *The Continuous Esteem of the Prophet's Family* by Sheikh Yusuf al-Nabhani (Sheikhy Notes, 2019). Imam Malik (may Allah show him mercy) maintains the position that he prefers Fatimah (may Allah be pleased with her) over all the Companions because she is a part of the Prophet (may Allah bestow peace and blessings upon him).

Aishah (may Allah be pleased with her) was the youngest of the wives of the Prophet (may Allah bestow peace and blessings upon him). The marriage was contractually agreed; however, it was not until she was fully mature that she lived with the Prophet (may Allah bestow peace and blessings upon him), which was several years later. She was to be married to someone else but that proposal broke down. Then the Prophet (may Allah be pleased with her) said that he wanted to marry her because he had seen three dreams with Aishah (may Allah be pleased with her) as his wife.

The Prophet (may Allah bestow peace and blessings upon him) said,

لا تؤذيني في عائشة، فإن الوحي لم ينزل علي في لحاف واحدة منكن غير عائشة

"Do not harm me by [harming] Aishah because revelation does not come down to me in the blanket of any of you except Aishah."[62] Perhaps it is for this reason that Abu Hanifah (may Allah show him mercy) preferred her over other women of the nation. In any case, no one should argue or debate which one is better than the other as they could be committing sins and not good works. Another reason for her virtue over others is the additional part at the end of the hadith of the complete women in which she is compared to a delicacy. And Allah knows best.

The Rawafid are a branch of the Shia who refused to support Zayd ibn 'Ali and yet claim to support Ahl al-Bayt!

---

[62] Bukhari 2581.

The Quran was revealed announcing Aishah's (may Allah be pleased with her) innocence beyond any doubt: "Those who came with the slander are a band of you; do not reckon it evil for you, rather [you think] it is good for you. Every man of them shall have the sin that he has earned charged to him, and whosoever of them took upon himself the greater part of it, for him there awaits a mighty chastisement. Why, when you heard it, did the believing men and women not of their own account think good thoughts, and say, 'This is a manifest calumny'? Why did they not bring four witnesses against it? But since they did not bring the witnesses, before Allah they are the liars."[63] These verses were revealed in the context about the false lies that were spread against Aishah (may Allah be pleased with her) and that Allah (the Exalted) Himself clarified the matter as slander and vindicated her. Backbiting is when the matter is true and slander when it is false. Some of the Shia still hang onto the slander and are therefore liars, according the very text of the Quran. Perhaps the reason they do this is because they oppose the first three caliphs and Aishah is the daughter of Abu Bakr (may Allah be pleased with them).

---

[63] Quran: al-Nur 11–21.

Residents of paradise and hell are in there forever

وأهل الجنة في الجنة خالدون وأهل النار في النار خالدون لقوله تعالى في حق المؤمنين أُولَئِكَ أَصْحَابُ الْجَنَّةِ هُمْ فِيهَا خَالِدُونَ وفي حق الكافرين أُولَئِكَ أَصْحَابُ النَّارِ هُمْ فِيهَا خَالِدُونَ

"The residents of paradise are in paradise forever and the residents of hell are in hell forever, in view of the Exalted having said about the believers, 'They are the dwellers of paradise and remain in it forever.'[64] And in regard to the disbelievers, 'They are the dwellers of hell and remain in it forever.'"[65]

Commentary

In regard to the residents of hell, Imam al-Samarqandi (may Allah show him mercy) said about the final word "forever", "they are in it permanently, they do not die and do not leave."

---

[64] Quran: al-Baqarah 2:82.
[65] Quran: al-Baqarah 2:81.

This verse is about disbelievers entering hell, that they do not leave. The believers could enter the fire for a period, which is limited. Then they will leave it to enter paradise. Disbelievers never enter paradise, because that abode is only for believers.

There is a famous disagreement about hell coming to an end. Ibn Taymiyyah said in his *al-Radd ‘ala Man Qala bi-Fana’ al-Jannah wa al-Nar* (*Refutation of Those Who Say Paradise and Hell End*),

وأما خلق نفوس تعمل الشر في الدنيا وفي الآخرة لا تكون إلا في العذاب، فهذا تناقض يظهر فيه من مناقضة الحكمة والرحمة ما لا يظهر في غيره

"As for creating souls to do evil in the world and in the afterlife that they just be for punishment, this contains manifest deficiency, in terms of wisdom and mercy, not present elsewhere" (p. 83).

He also mentions that the Ash‘aris do not understand mercy. So it is quite easy to refute him. Allah (the Exalted) has warned mankind about hell several times and has given them numerous occasions in their lives to reflect and realise that our lives are not meaningless. Allah (the Exalted) does not force anyone to commit a sin or commit disbelief – that is their choice alone. It is not the Ash'aris who did not understand mercy; rather, it is Ibn Taymiyyah who did not understand that mercy is only shown to the believers in the afterlife. There is no mercy for disbelievers after they die.

Imam Taqi al-Din al-Subki (d. 756 AH) said, "The faith of Muslims is that paradise and hell do not perish, Abu Muhammad ibn Hazm having transmitted scholarly consensus (*ijma'*) on this point and on the fact that whoever denies it is an unbeliever (*kafir*) by scholarly consensus. And there is no doubt of this, for it is necessarily known ['necessarily known' meaning things that any Muslim should know about if asked] as part of the religion of Islam, and proof after proof bears it out. Allah Most High says: (1) 'Nay, but whoever earns a wicked deed and is encompassed by his error, those are the inhabitants of hell, abiding therein forever' (Koran 2:81)."[66]

There are fifty-six Quranic verses which corroborate that hell is eternal: 2:162, 3:116, 4:14, 4:93, 4:168–9, 6:128, 7:36, 9:63, 9:68, 10:27, 11:106–7, 13:5, 16:29, 21:99, 23:103, 32:14, 25:69, 33:64–5, 39:72, 41:28, 43:74–5, 47:15,

---

[66] Sheikh Nuh Ha Mim Keller, *Reliance of the Traveller* (Amana Publications, 1991) pp. 995–1002 (w55.3).

59:17, 64:10, 72:23, 98:6, 2:86, 32:20, 2:167, 2:102, 3:22, 4:56, 4:121, 5:37, 11:8, 11:16, 14:21, 14:29, 23:108, 29:23, 45:35, 22:22, 35:36, 17:97, 40:49–50, 42:45, 69:36, 78:30, 87:13, 90:20, 82:16.[67]

There are thirty-eight verses about paradise being eternal: 2:82, 3:15, 10:62, 3:198, 4:13, 4:57, 5:85, 5:119, 9:89, 9:100, 11:23, 10:26, 11:108, 13:35, 14:23, 15:48, 18:3, 18:107, 20:76, 21:102, 23:11, 25:15, 25:76, 29:58, 4:122, 39:73, 41:8, 43:71, 41:30, 48:5, 56:17, 57:12, 58:22, 50:34, 64:9, 65:11, 95:6, 98:8.[68]

Imam al-Taftazani (may Allah show him mercy) said in *al-'Aqa'id al-Nasafiyyah*,

وذهب الجهمية إلى أنهما يفنيان ويفنى أهلهما، وهو قول باطل مخالف للكتاب والسنة والإجماع، ليس عليه شبهة فضلاً عن الحجة

"Al-Jahamiyyah maintain that they [i.e. paradise and hell] end, which is a baseless opinion that opposes the Quran, Sunnah and scholarly consensus (*ijma'*). There is no doubt whatsoever

---

[67] Ibid., p. 996.
[68] Ibid., p. 997.

[on this matter] such that it should require evidence." Jahamiyyah is another name for the Mu'tazilites because the main voice for this group was Jahm ibn Safwan.

Al-Manawi (may Allah show him mercy) said in *Fayd al-Qadir*,

و هذا صريح في أن الجنة أبدية لا تفنى والنار مثلها، وزعم جهم بن صفوان أنهما فانيتان لأنهما حادثتان، ولم يتابعه أحد من الإسلاميين بل كفروه به، وذهب بعضهم إلى إفناء النار دون الجنة وأطال ابن القيم كشيخه ابن تيمية في الإنتصار له في عدة كراريس، وقد صار بذلك أقرب إلى الكفر منه إلى الإيمان لمخالفته نص القرءان، وختم بذلك كتابه الذي في وصف الجنان

"It is clear that paradise is eternal and hell does not end similarly. Jahm ibn Safwan claims they end and they come into being, though not one of the Islamic scholars agreed with him; rather, they said it was disbelief. Some of them hold the opinion that hell ends but not paradise. Ibn Qayyim has the same opinion as his teacher Ibn Taymiyyah by supporting him in a number of booklets. So by this he is closer to disbelief than he was to faith because he opposed the Quran. He ends his book with that description of paradise."

There are more texts that can be quoted and this is not a surprise. Some say that they do not believe that Abu Hanifah (may Allah show him mercy) could make such statements because it was not an issue except many centuries later. For me this is a miracle of Abu Hanifah (may Allah show him mercy) and it was advice for his students to look beyond this world and look for our permanent life.

وما رواه الشيخان عن ابن عمر رضي الله عنهما قال: قال رسول الله صلى الله عليه وسلم: إذا صار أهل الجنة إلى الجنة وأهل النار إلى النار جيء بالموت حتى يجعلَ بين الجنة والنار، ثم يُذبحُ، ثم يُنادي منادٍ: يا أهل الجنة لا موتَ، يا أهل النار لا موتَ، فيزدادُ أهل الجنة فرحًا إلى فرحهم، ويزداد أهل النار جزئًا إلى حزنهم

"It was reported from the two scholars [Bukhari and Muslim] from Ibn ʿUmar (may Allah be

140

pleased with them) who reports that the Messenger of Allah (may Allah bestow peace and blessings upon him) said, 'When the residents of paradise go to paradise and the residents of hell go to hell, death will be brought between heaven and hell, and then it will sacrificed. Then a caller will proclaim, "O residents of paradise, no death. O resident of hell, no death." The residents of paradise increase in unbound happiness and the residents of hell increase in unbound sorrow.'"

Death takes the form of a ram, which is sacrificed, and then there is no death. The residents of hell remain in hell forever and the residents of heaven remain in there forever. This is after those who who have the smallest part of faith in their hearts have been taken out of hell. If people are to remain in paradise and hell forever, the place they remain in must necessarily be forever.

Closing

والحمد لله رب العالمين وحده وصلى الله على
سيدنا محمد وعلى آله وصحبه أجمعين

"All praise belongs to Allah alone, Lord of all
creation, and peace and blessings be upon our
master Muhammad and upon all his family and
Companions."

Commentary

All religious texts begin with praise of Allah and
invoking blessings and peace upon the Prophet
(may Allah bestow peace and blessings upon him).
According to Imam al-Nawawi adding "our
master" is permitted in the *tashahhud* as it is here.
Here the invocations precede the praise of Allah
(the Exalted) whereas it is normally the praise of
Allah followed by the invocations. Included are the
Prophetic family and Companions because this is
an important part of Ahl al-Sunnah veneration. The
respect due to both parties constitutes what Ahl al-
Sunnah stands for, while following one and
ignoring the other is what sects do. The Shia claim
to follow the family and the Wahhabis claim to

142

follow the Companions. Neither are correct in their approach of abandoning some and adopting others.

تمت وصية الإمام أبي حنيفة لأصحابه رضي الله تعالى عنهم أجمعين أمين أمين أمين وأفضل الصلاة وأزكى التسليم على سيدنا محمد وعلى آله وصحبه أجمعين والحمد لله وحده

"The *Wasiyyah* of Imam Abu Hanifah to his students is hereby complete. May Allah be pleased with them all, *amin*, *amin*, *amin*, and may the most virtuous of prayers, and purest of blessings, be upon our master Muhammad and upon his all family and Companions. And all praise belongs to Allah alone."

This completes the commentary and translation of the *Wasiyyah* of Imam Abu Hanifah (may Allah show him mercy), on 28 Sha'ban 1441 / 22 April 2020.

Printed in Great Britain
by Amazon